Value
Merchants

Also by the Authors

JAMES C. ANDERSON AND
JAMES A. NARUS

*Business Market Management: Understanding,
Creating, and Delivering Value,* 2nd ed.
(Upper Saddle River, NJ: Pearson Prentice Hall, 2004).

NIRMALYA KUMAR

*Marketing as Strategy: Understanding the CEO's
Agenda for Driving Growth and Innovation*
(Boston: Harvard Business School Press, 2004).

NIRMALYA KUMAR AND
JAN-BENEDICT E. M. STEENKAMP

*Private Label Strategy: How to Meet
the Store Brand Challenge*
(Boston: Harvard Business School Press, 2007).

Value Merchants

Demonstrating and Documenting
Superior Value in Business Markets

James C. Anderson
Nirmalya Kumar
James A. Narus

HARVARD BUSINESS SCHOOL PRESS
Boston, Massachusetts

Library of Congress Cataloging-in-Publication Data
Anderson, James C., 1953–
   Value merchants: demonstrating and documenting superior value in
business markets / James C. Anderson, Nirmalya Kumar, and James A. Narus.
      p.   cm.
   ISBN-13: 978-1-4221-0335-7 (hardcover: alk. paper)
   ISBN-10: 1-4221-0335-8
   1. Industrial marketing. 2. Sales promotion. 3. Purchasing. I. Kumar,
Nirmalya. II. Narus, James A. III. Title.
   HF5415.1263.A534 2007
   658.8'04—dc22
                                                    2007017289

To my sons Perry and Ross:

so challenging, so worthwhile . . .

so much love.

—JCA

To Vijay Mittal—

value merchant and

invaluable friend.

—NK

To Simon and Genevieve Narus

for a lifetime of support and

encouragement.

—JAN

CONTENTS

PREFACE

WE HAVE WRITTEN this book for general managers, marketing managers, and sales managers whose businesses serve business markets—firms, institutions, and governments. A common lament that we hear from these managers is that although they believe their offerings deliver superior value to customers, their businesses have difficulty persuading customers of this. Customer managers, increasingly pressed for time and demonstrable results, appear to focus simply on reducing price. What causes this? A faulty customer value proposition? A lack of knowledge of how to persuasively substantiate the superior value of their offerings relative to those offered by competitors? Salespeople who are unwilling, or unable, to sell value and instead rely on price concessions to retain or gain business? Each of these may contribute to frustrating results, when sales may grow but profitability lags disappointingly behind.

Our book enables general managers, marketing managers, and sales managers to overcome such obstacles and get a better return on the superior value that their market offerings deliver to target customers. We contend that to prosper in today's demanding business markets, supplier managers have to fundamentally reexamine their philosophy of doing business and how they put it into practice. Suppliers must adopt a philosophy of doing business based on demonstrated and documented superior value and implement that philosophy using an approach we call *customer value management*. Customer value management is a progressive, practical approach to business markets that, in its essence, has two basic goals:

1. Deliver superior value to targeted market segments and customer firms

2. Get an equitable return on the value delivered

Customer value management relies on customer value assessment to gain an understanding of customer requirements and preferences and what fulfilling those are worth in monetary terms. Although firms may be able to accomplish the first goal without any methodical assessment of customer value, it is unlikely that they will be able to accomplish the second goal without it. Simply put, to gain an equitable or fair return on the value their offerings deliver, suppliers must be able to persuasively demonstrate and document the superior value they provide customers relative to the next-best alternative.

In this book we provide readers with a detailed, step-by-step understanding of customer value management and how to implement it in their businesses. We begin with how to conceptualize value and go all the way through to how to profit from the superior value provided. We offer numerous case examples from businesses in a wide variety of industries and countries to support our approach and help bring it to life for readers. In writing this book, we also draw on our experience in working with companies over the past decade to implement customer value management. We have seen the significant contribution that customer value management can make to business performance. Isn't it time for your business to really profit from superior customer value?

ACKNOWLEDGMENTS

M ANY INDIVIDUALS and organizations have provided support to enable us to write this book. While we are grateful to them all, we single out some of them here to explicitly acknowledge their contributions.

We first want to thank the many managers who so graciously took time out of their busy schedules to talk with us. The best practices that these managers shared with us made an enormous contribution. In particular, we would like to especially acknowledge:

Nada El-Zein, Akzo Nobel

Elisa Scarletta and Mark Stoneburner, Applied Industrial Technologies

Eric Berggren and Stefanie Zucker, Axios Partners

Steve Dehmlow, Composites One

Michael Lanham, Dow Corning

Alice Griffin and Robert Smith, Eastman Chemical

Robb Kristopher and Debra Oler, Grainger

Frank Joop, Intergraph

Joy Chandler and John Stang, Kennametal

Marcel de Nooijer and Eelco van Asch, KLM Cargo

Gene Lowe, Milliken

Bas Beckers and Bert Willemsen, Orange Orca

William Blankemeier, PeopleFlo Manufacturing

Art Helmstetter, Quaker Chemical

Joe Razum, Rockwell Automation (now Baldor)

Siva Mahasandana and Chantana Sukumanont, Siam City Cement

Todd Snelgrove, SKF

Eddie L. Smith, Sonoco

Michael Butkovic and Jackie Eckey, Swagelok

Peeyush Gupta and Anand Sen, Tata Steel

We want to thank the Institute for the Study of Business Markets (ISBM), located at Penn State University, for its financial support of our management practice research. We especially want to acknowledge Ralph Oliva, the executive director of ISBM, and Gary Lilien, the research director of ISBM, for their support of our work.

We also want to express our gratitude to Kirsten Sandberg of Harvard Business School Press for her support and editorial guidance of the project.

James C. Anderson would like to thank his research associates at the Kellogg School of Management—Chaitali Bhagdev, Abhinav Gattani, and Akshaya Gulhati—for their capable assistance in this project. He would also like to thank his assistant, James Ward, for James's helpful suggestions and skillful assistance in constructing the figures and tables.

Nirmalya Kumar gratefully acknowledges the following companies and individuals who over the years were kind enough to allow him to test his ideas regarding value in business markets: ACC, Aditya Birla Group (Kumaramanglam Birla, Santrupt Misra), Akzo Nobel, Alcan, Alfred McAlpine, AT&T, Bekaert, Bertelsmann Direct Group (Gerd Bührig, Ewald Walgenbach), BT (Tim Evans, Gavin Patterson), Caterpillar, Chilton, Continental,

Dow Chemical (Carlos Silva Lopes), DuPont, Essel Propack (Ashok Goel), Goodyear, Ambuja Cements, Hewlett-Packard, Holcim (Markus Akermann, Paul Hugentobler), Hydro Aluminum, IBM, ICI, ISS, Jardine Matheson, Jotun, Motorola, Nokia, Norwegian Post, Orkla Group (Karin Aslaksen, Ole Enger), RPG Enterprises (Pradipto Mohaptra), Sabic, Shell, Schindler, Tetra Pak, Volvo, WPP Group (Mark Read), and Zensar Technologies (Ganesh Natarajan). He also thanks his colleagues at London Business School and the associate director of the Aditya Birla India Center, Suseela Yesudian-Storfjell.

James A. Narus thanks the following companies and managers for their assistance with this project: W.R. Grace (Larry Golen), Okuma America (Seth Machlus), Sonoco (Vicki Arthur, Greg Powell), Timken Corporation (Brian Berg), and Volvo Trucks (Clay Flynt).

Developed with the support of the Institute for
the Study of Business Markets at Penn State.

Institute for
the Study of
Business Markets

ONE

Value Merchants

Doing Business on Demonstrably Superior Value

A SUPPLIER OF integrated circuits (ICs) for correcting power input was competing for the business of an electronic device manufacturer, which was projecting a demand of 5 million units for incorporation into its next-generation device. In the course of the negotiation, the supplier's salesperson learned that he was competing against another firm whose price for the integrated circuits was 10¢ lower per IC—45¢ versus 35¢. The customer asked the salespeople from both firms to explain the source of the superior value for their offering relative to the competing offering. This particular salesperson replied that it was his personal and dedicated servicing of the account.

Unbeknownst to him, the customer had built a customer value model in which it had found that his offering, though 10¢ higher in price, was actually worth 15.9¢ more than the alternative supplier. Further, the electronics engineer who was leading the development project had recommended to the purchasing manager supporting the project that he purchase those ICs, even at the higher price. The salesperson's personal and dedicated servicing as a favorable point of difference was worth something in the model—0.2¢! Unfortunately, the salesperson overlooked the two elements providing the greatest differential value, apparently unaware of the magnitude of the differences and what those differences were worth to that customer. As expected, when push came to shove in the negotiations with purchasing, the salesperson gave a 10¢ price concession to match the competitor's price and "win" the business (perhaps he suspected that his superior service was not worth the 10¢ difference after all). The result? The firm lost $500,000 (5 million units at 10¢) of potential profit on a single transaction!

Talk to seasoned general managers or business unit executives in business markets, and they will recount a similar story in which:

- Their salespeople have a poor understanding of what really creates value for customers.

- Their business makes vague promises of superior value without any supporting data.

- Salespeople frequently play the role of *value spendthrifts*, giving value away through price concessions to make the sale, rather than *value merchants*, who sell profitable growth by stressing the superior value of the firm's offerings.

- Despite providing greater value than competitors, their business is forced to compete as a commodity and therefore does not get a fair return from its superior value.

The result, as in the case just examined, is that even though the supplier believed that its products and services had greater value than those of the next-best alternative, it ended up matching competitor prices. "Leaving money on the table," as this supplier did, has a direct and substantial negative impact on the supplier's profitability. Why does this happen as often as it does in business markets?

Purchasing managers in business markets are becoming increasingly sophisticated in their strategies and tactics. Increasingly held accountable for reducing costs, purchasing and other customer managers don't have the luxury of simply believing suppliers' claims of cost savings. A relatively easy and quick way to obtain savings is for purchasing managers to focus on price and obtain price concessions from suppliers. To enhance their negotiating power, purchasing managers attempt to convince suppliers that their offerings are the same as their competitors—that they could be easily replaced. In the face of such pressure, as the IC example illustrates, suppliers cave in and match competitor prices. It is a rare commodity in business markets to find firms that do business based on demonstrably superior value.

Senior managers of companies serving business markets—that is, firms, institutions, or governments—are frustrated that they often are cast as "commodity" suppliers. Their customers have been effective in demanding more but have been unwilling to pay for it. As the need to cut costs in companies continues, the pricing pressure that such customers place on their suppliers is not likely to abate. Thus, business as usual—or even doing more of the same with less, which is a common response—will not provide solutions worth pursuing.

Customer Value Management: A Progressive, Practical Approach

To combat price concessions and commoditization pressures, firms have to fundamentally reexamine their philosophy of doing business and how they put it into practice. Suppliers must adopt a philosophy of doing business based on demonstrated and documented superior value and implement that philosophy using an approach we call *customer value management*. Customer value management is a progressive, practical approach to business markets that, in its essence, has two basic goals:

1. Deliver superior value to targeted market segments and customer firms

2. Get an equitable return on the value delivered

Customer value management relies on customer value assessment to gain an understanding of customer requirements and preferences and what fulfilling those are worth in monetary terms. Although firms may be able to accomplish the first goal without any systematic assessment of customer value, it is unlikely that they will be able to accomplish the second goal without it. Simply put, to gain an equitable or fair return on the value their offerings deliver, suppliers must be able to persuasively demonstrate and document the superior value they provide customers relative to the next-best alternative.

"Green" Money Versus "Gray" Money

Senior managers at most firms in business markets have come to realize that if they can cut the cost of acquired goods and services, such procurement savings will fall to the bottom line as improved profitability. Thus, nearly every firm has set goals for purchasing to cut the cost of acquired goods and services. These goals are typically expressed as total cost reduction goals and tend to take one of two forms. They may be expressed as a targeted cost reduction amount, such as reducing the cost of acquired goods and services by $2 billion over three years (as one oil company did), or as a yearly percentage reduction, such as reducing costs by 10 percent, 5 percent, and 5 percent over three consecutive years (as one automotive manufacturer did). However, the translation of these goals into purchasing practice often leads to a bias that one purchasing director captured with the expression "green money versus gray money." What did he mean by that?

Green money (the predominant color of U.S. currency) refers to cost savings for which purchasing managers can readily get credit, whereas *gray money* refers to cost savings that are difficult for them to claim. Getting three bids, picking the lowest one, and then negotiating a further price reduction is green money. It reflects directly on purchasing's contribution to the goal that senior management has set. Acquiring an offering that provides a lower total cost of ownership but that may have a higher purchase price is gray money. Because of limited time and measurement capabilities, a purchasing manager may not be able to document that she has actually received the cost savings that the supplier assured her firm.

But it doesn't have to be that way. A manufacturer of controls for automating manufacturing lines has its salespeople spend time at prospective customers gathering data on what controls would be required, what the total cost of them would be (not just purchase price, but all costs, such as installation and training), and what the payback period would be if the customer were to purchase them. The salesperson pulls this research together into a report that demonstrates the potential savings, which he then provides to the prospective customer. Whose name appears on the cover of the report? The purchasing manager's. The supplier salesperson's name appears nowhere on the cover of the report. Now, the purchasing manager can take this report to her senior management and say, "Look, I have been doing some research in conjunction with this supplier, and this is how we can save some money." What has this supplier done? Enabled the purchasing manager to turn gray money into green money. It also has provided another benefit: allowing the purchasing manager to leverage her time, which is in short supply.

Demonstrating and Documenting Superior Value

Increasingly, to get an equitable or fair return, suppliers must be able to persuasively demonstrate and document the superior value their offerings deliver to customers. By "demonstrate," we mean showing prospective customers convincingly beforehand what cost savings or added value they can expect from using the supplier's offering relative to the next-best alternative. Value case histories are one tool that best-practice suppliers, such as Nijdra Groep in the Netherlands and Rockwell Automation, use to accomplish this. *Value case histories* are written accounts that document the cost savings or added value that reference customers have received from using a supplier's market offering. Another way that best-practice firms, such as GE Infrastructure Water & Process Technologies and SKF, demonstrate the value of their offerings to prospective customers is through customer value assessment tools, which we term *value calculators*. These tools are spreadsheet software applications that salespeople or value specialists conduct on laptops as part of a consultative selling approach to demonstrate the value that customers likely would receive from their offerings.

Demonstrating superior value is necessary, but it is no longer enough to become a best-practice company in today's business markets. Suppliers also must document the cost savings and incremental profits that offerings have delivered to customers. Thus, suppliers work with their customers to define the measures on which they will track the cost savings or incremental profit produced and then, after a suitable period of time, work with customer managers to substantiate the results.

Documenting the superior value delivered to customers provides four powerful benefits to suppliers. First, it enhances the credibility of the value demonstrations for their offerings because customer managers know that the supplier is willing to return later to document the value received. Second, documenting enables customer managers to get credit for the cost savings and incremental profit produced. Third, documenting enables suppliers to create value case histories and other materials for use in marketing communications to persuasively convey to prospective customers the value they, too, might obtain from the supplier's offering. Finally, by comparing the value actually delivered with the value claimed in the demonstration and regressing these differences on customer descriptors, documenting enables suppliers to further refine their understanding of how their offerings deliver the greatest value. This sharpens subsequent efforts to target customers. We term the tools that suppliers use to document the value of their offerings *value documenters*.

For a moment, put yourself in the role of a commercial grower. Two suppliers are offering you mulch film, which is a thin plastic sheet that commercial growers place on the ground to hold in moisture, prevent weed growth, and allow vegetables and melons to be planted closer together. One supplier comes to you with this proposition: "Trust us. Our mulch film will lower your cost." The other supplier, Sonoco, comes to you with this proposition: "Sonoco just lowered the cost of your mulch film by $16.83 per acre." *And* Sonoco offers to show you exactly how it determined that figure. Which supplier's value proposition is more persuasive?

How Customer Value Management Leads to Success

Before pursuing a proposed approach that changes the way of doing business, senior management wants to know why it's more likely to succeed than others After all, achieving any enduring change in a business is very difficult. So what are the unique strengths in an approach that make it worth pursuing? Customer value management has three unique strengths: superior conceptualization of value, a progressive approach to assessing value in practice, and proven concepts and tools for translating knowledge of customer value into superior business performance.

Superior conceptualization of customer value. To achieve success, senior managers need a conceptualization of customer value that they and their managers, salespeople, and business customers can readily grasp and find reasonable. Despite all the writing and talk about customer value in business markets, we contend that there has not been a reasoned, understandable conceptualization. As a result, there is substantial variation in what is meant by "customer value" in business markets, which has hindered implementing assessments of it.

We provide a comprehensive, well-reasoned conceptualization of customer value in chapter 2. It expresses customer value in the same metric as we ask customers to make purchase decisions (monetary terms, not importance ratings). It specifies what is and what is *not* value (e.g., price). Finally, our expression of the fundamental value equation especially lends itself to assessment in practice and reflects how customers decide between competing offerings.

Progressive approach to assessing value in practice. Approaches to assessing customer value that are cumbersome in practice or that require statistics experts will be met with resistance, especially from the sales force and customers. Total cost of ownership, for example, is hard to argue with as a concept. The problem is that it proves to be unworkable in practice. Customers have limited patience in cooperating with suppliers because customer managers have greater responsibility and increasing demands on their time. Where once a manager at a particular level might have had responsibility for $10 million in business, he may now have responsibility for $50 million. Customers also have a limited willingness to share their data with suppliers. Each of these facts works against the meticulous, time-consuming process of gathering data to estimate the total cost or, better still, total value of ownership in practice. As a result, efforts devolve into compromising shortcuts—such as filling out forms, guessing, and recycling opinions—in place of actually gathering data.[1]

In contrast, each aspect of our approach to assessing customer value has been developed and refined in working with suppliers across a diverse array of industries. Our approach to customer value assessment focuses the supplier's and customers' limited resources on the *value elements*—that is, the specific ways the offerings reduce customer costs or enable the customer to earn additional revenue and profit—that matter most and assessing them in the way that matters most. As we detail in chapters 2 and 3, we take a measurement approach that precisely defines the value elements, stating the data needed to estimate each one. We emphasize data gathering and minimize the role perception plays. The guiding principle is to generate new knowledge, not recycle opinion. Thus, a litmus test for our approach is this: are the supplier and the customers that participate in the research more knowledgeable about how the supplier's offering adds value or reduces cost in the customer's business than what they were before the research? Our approach enables marketing and sales to significantly contribute to competing on analytics and evidence-based management.[2]

Proven concepts and tools for achieving superior business performance. Our work with many clients and more than ten years of management practice research have enabled us to discover, devise, and refine concepts and tools that, when implemented with integrity, lead to superior business performance—like devising customer value propositions that resonate with target customers; constructing and deploying value-based sales tools that the sales force is able to use and wants to use; and pursuing new knowledge with the intent of better understanding what will lead to superior business performance. We want to make it clear that there is no trickery, deception, or sleight of hand in customer value management. Rather, it is fundamental thinking proven in practice to significantly improve business performance. Throughout this book, and especially in chapter 8, we provide proof points of how suppliers practicing what we advocate have achieved superior business performance. We begin with the experience of Sonoco in the next section.

Enhancing Business Performance with Customer Value Management

Ultimately, there are three basic sales approaches prevalent in business markets. First is selling on price. Most firms are, however, not set up to sell on price because it requires relentless cost cutting, moving production overseas to low-cost locations, and trading low margins for (hopefully) higher volume. In this type of commodity business, purchasing managers tend to dominate customer interactions, and suppliers have little pricing flexibility. Suppliers can attempt to compete on price, but how many suppliers in a given market can have the lowest price? Just one. Not willing to accept this basic fact, suppliers pursue business through price cutting, often orchestrated by adroit purchasing managers.

To escape this exclusive focus on price, most suppliers pursue a second approach: they claim that they provide superior value— and deserve to be compensated appropriately. Unfortunately for the suppliers, most often this translates into "Trust us, our offerings are worth more." The claims of superior value are just that— claims! These value assertions are not substantiated by any in-depth analysis on the part of the supplier and therefore cannot be demonstrated nor documented to customers. The result is that suppliers have little choice but to end up competing on price when pressed by purchasing managers. As shown in the IC case, this does not mean that the supplier is not providing superior value; it's just that the supplier lacks the ability to prove its claims. Even if the supplier and the customer agree that the supplier's offering delivers greater value than the competitor's offering, they may have substantially different opinions of what this greater value is worth in monetary terms to the customer.

This brings us to the third approach, which we recommend and develop in this book. Customer value management is a data-driven approach to demonstrating and documenting in monetary terms the superior value that a supplier's offerings deliver to customers. Competing on price may work if the company has the lowest cost in the industry and chooses to pass it along to customers instead of using this advantage to build differences that are valuable to target customers. But, for most companies, customer value management is a more viable way to enhance business performance. Surprisingly, though, only a few progressive companies follow this approach. Let's consider the experience of Sonoco.

Sonoco: Achieving Superior Business Performance

The CEO of Sonoco, Harris DeLoach Jr., and his executive committee have set an ambitious growth goal for the firm: double-digit, sustainable, profitable growth every year. DeLoach and the executive committee believe that adopting the customer value management approach is crucial for achieving such growth. Thus, DeLoach has championed a distinctive value propositions (DVPs) program, giving responsibility for its implementation to Eddie Smith, vice president of strategy and business development and a member of the executive committee. Smith has established that Sonoco DVPs must fulfill three criteria:

1. *Distinctive*—Sonoco's value proposition must be superior to that of its competition.

2. *Measurable*—Sonoco prefers that all value propositions are based on tangible points of difference that can be quantified in monetary terms.

3. *Sustainable*—Sonoco will be able to execute this value proposition for as long as possible.

Although it's not on the list, Smith adds the requirement that all Sonoco value propositions be "translated into the customer's unique language." By that, he means that sales and marketing people must be able to identify what's in it for the customer.

The executive team has signaled how critical DVPs are to business unit performance by making value propositions the first of ten different metrics on the performance scorecard for which general managers are accountable. In senior management reviews, business unit general managers present the value proposition for each of their target market segments and key customers. Every presented value proposition is scored on the three criteria for DVPs. The general manager then receives summary feedback on the value proposition metric (as well as on each of the other nine growth factors) as follows:

- *Green*—capable of meeting the profitable growth goal

- *Yellow*—prompting significant concerns that need to be addressed

- *Red*—not adequate to meet the profitable growth goal

Not content to rely simply on belief, Sonoco senior management has had data gathered to understand the relation between business units' value propositions and their performance. Sonoco has found that there is a significant positive relation. Further, it has found that improvement in DVPs leads to improved business unit performance.

Has Sonoco been able to achieve the overall growth goal that senior management sought, in part, through its use of customer value management and DVPs? Sonoco sales increased 14.4 percent from 2003 to 2004, 11.8 percent from 2004 to 2005, and 4.1 percent from 2005 to 2006, for a three-year average sales growth of 10.1 percent. Perhaps more important, profitability expressed as earnings before interest and taxes (EBIT) increased 23.9 percent from 2003 to 2004, 14.6 percent from 2004 to 2005, and 17.6 percent from 2005 to 2006, for a three-year average growth in EBIT of 18.7 percent. While superior business performance depends on a number of factors, Sonoco's experience provides strong evidence that customer value management makes a significant contribution.

Promoting a Value-Driven Philosophy to Business Markets

The responsibility for leading a value-based market strategy in business markets lies at the top of the firm. Senior managers need to convey to the firm that it generates value through both its core offerings and its augmenting services and that it expects to receive an equitable return for those offerings and services. In larger multi-business firms, the senior management of each business unit—especially the general manager and top marketing and sales executives—has primary responsibility for customer value management. We will show that customer value management is more than a marketing and sales activity, so the general manager must ultimately own and lead its successful implementation.

While "senior management support" may sound like a cliché, we have found through both outstanding and terrible experiences while working with firms to implement customer value management that it is no cliché—it's absolutely essential. And such support cannot be simply talk from senior managers about how important customer value management is. More telling to everyone in the business is how senior managers choose to spend their time. Making time in their schedules to attend the launch of customer value management initiatives, serving as executive sponsors of customer value projects, monitoring the progress of initiatives, and setting aside a day to attend business cases for change and to give feedback all send a stronger message throughout the business that senior management is committed to implementing a philosophy of doing business based on demonstrated and documented value to customers.

Sonoco's corporate culture reinforces to each salesperson the preeminence of value in the firm's overall market strategy. From the day they are hired, sales representatives learn that Sonoco products are typically higher priced than those of competitors. And they quickly discover that Sonoco prospers because it provides value to its customers in the form of technologically superior products and outstanding services. From these lessons, salespersons readily conclude that if they are to succeed at Sonoco, they must sell value, not price. Moreover, the Sonoco "value story" is repeatedly reinforced through such things as annual reports, brochures, company newsletters, case histories presented at sales meetings, and sales tools.

GE Infrastructure Water & Process Technologies (W&PT), for example, stresses the importance of documenting the results its solutions have provided customers in its brand slogan: "Proof, not Promises." What does this slogan mean? According to W&PT's

Web site, "'Proof, not Promises' is the GE Water Technologies commitment to measure success in terms of the savings and performance improvements achieved for our customers. 'Proof, not Promises' sets a standard for excellence and accountability that our customers can count on, providing documented proof that their profitability goals have been met."

Similarly signaling its commitment to documenting the results it delivers to customers, Sweden's SKF, a global leader in bearings, has given its SKF Documented Solutions Program this tagline: "Real world savings—and we can prove it!" Figure 1-1 illustrates SKF's customer value approach.

Of course, Sonoco, W&PT, SKF, and the other best-practice firms we will draw on in this book did not just stumble onto customer value management. Their journeys began years ago with small steps, learning through experience, and an unwavering, visible commitment by senior management to see the approach through. We find that despite all the talk about value in business markets these days, these leaders are in the minority. In fact, remarkably few suppliers have made any systematic or methodical effort to understand the value of their offerings to customers. They talk about value but continue to struggle against commoditization pressures and succumb repeatedly to customer demands for price concessions. However, by adopting customer value management as a philosophy for doing business, suppliers can demonstrate and document the value of their offerings, helping turn gray money into green money for both customers and themselves.

Overview of the Book: The Path to Superior Business Profitability

Our intent in this book is to transform businesses and, especially, their sales forces into value merchants. Doing business based on demonstrating and documenting superior value is, indeed, a rare commodity. Yet it doesn't have to be so rare. We contend that by

FIGURE 1-1

SKF Documented Solutions program advertisement

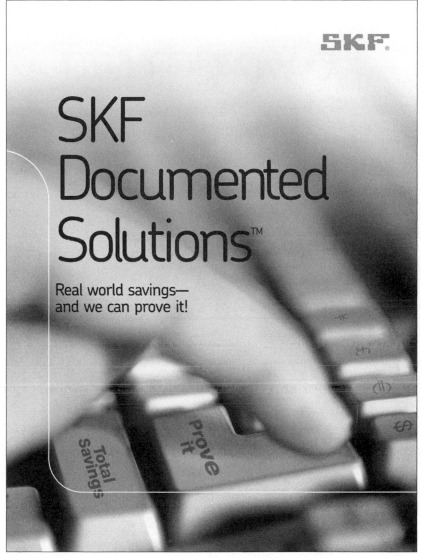

(continued)

FIGURE 1-1 (continued)

SKF Documented Solutions program description

How much can SKF save you?

Let's do the numbers.

Introducing SKF Documented Solutions*

SKF® is probably not the first of your supplier partners to talk about "documented savings." But we are confident that no one else can match the new tool we've developed for predicting the real-world, annual net cost savings you could realize from SKF products and services. An extension of our global "Real Conditions/Real Solutions" strategy, SKF Documented Solutions can show you how to cut thousands, if not hundreds of thousands of dollars, from your total operating budget.

Explore options and calculate savings.

At the heart of the SKF Documented Solution Program is powerful new proprietary software that draws on years of industry-specific experience and real-world performance data to "prove" savings in advance. In about one hour with an SKF representative, you can see precisely how a particular SKF solution can reduce your total cost of operation. And because the program allows you to plug in your own numbers—for materials, labor, downtime, energy costs, etc.—you can have confidence in the forecasted savings.

Based on industry-specific successes.

With nearly 100 years of experience, SKF knows a lot about your industry—the technical challenges you face, and how they can affect productivity and profitability. The SKF Documented Solution Program uses SKF's significant experience in your industry to document the viability of specific savings solutions. You'll see the actual, bottom-line results of similar solutions implemented by other companies in your industry.

Source: Provided courtesy of SKF USA Inc. Used with permission.

adopting the customer value management approach we present in this book, value merchants can prevail when they encounter challenges of the type that the IC salesperson faced. Specifically, readers of our book will learn how to:

- Assess customer value in practice

- Craft value propositions that resonate with target customers

- Achieve spirited implementation for superior profits

By embracing customer value management, readers can employ it in their own firms to drive superior business performance, just as the best-practice firms mentioned throughout this book have. We sketch the processes composing our customer value management approach in figure 1-2. The figure places the processes in sequence, which also serves as an overview of our book. We devote a chapter to detailing each of these constituent parts of customer value management.

Chapter 2 focuses on how to conceptualize value, which is the fundamental building block of customer value management, and addresses questions like these: What do we mean specifically by "value" in business markets? How does one define points of difference, points of parity, and points of contention vis-à-vis the

FIGURE 1-2

Customer value management processes

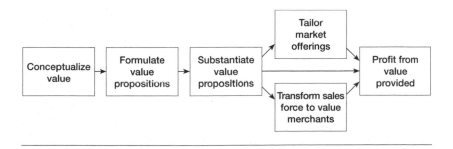

next-best alternative? What are the three types of value propositions suppliers use in business markets, and why is a value proposition with a resonating focus preferred over the other two?

Chapter 3 describes a process for firms to formulate their value propositions. It begins with analyzing what potential changes in the market offering customers would value most vis-à-vis the next-best alternative. This is used to develop a value proposition to aspire to. Then qualitative research is conducted to refine the value proposition. Finally, value word equations are developed to capture the points of difference in terms that customers can readily understand.

Chapter 4 provides a methodology for persuasively substantiating value propositions to customers. The value word equations are brought to life with data that is gathered in a customer value assessment. They are then used to construct value calculators that demonstrate the value to customers. Finally, value case histories and value documenters help prove to customers that they did indeed receive the value that the supplier promised them.

Chapter 5 demonstrates how a deep understanding of customer value can be used to tailor market offerings. Instead of the usual vanilla approach that provides the same bundle of products and services to all customer firms, a supplier can offer flexible market offerings. This allows more refined targeting through various levels of service and enables suppliers to capitalize on differences between customers.

Chapter 6 challenges suppliers to transform their sales forces from selling on price to becoming value merchants. While getting sales compensation aligned with selling on value and profit is critical, it is not enough. Businesses must foster value merchants and put a value-selling process and value-based sales tools in place. They must ensure initial and ongoing value-selling experiences with customers and instill and invigorate a value merchant culture.

Chapter 7 is all about how companies can profit from the superior value they provide customers. Although it is natural to think first of price premiums, there are also three other means of obtaining a fair return from customers for value provided in business markets. However, getting a fair return requires the supplier to manage pricing as if profitability depended on it! To accomplish this, we provide a value-based approach to pricing at the strategic, tactical, and transactional levels.

In chapter 8, we take up the challenge of prospering in business markets. We discuss what customer value management can and cannot do to help businesses prosper. We provide further evidence of the contribution it can make to superior business performance and consider how businesses can get started in implementing customer value management and becoming value merchants. Finally, we discuss how businesses that are value merchants can continue to provide superior value and profit from it.

The customer value management approach we present in this book provides state-of-the-art thinking, supported throughout by best practice from a variety of businesses, industries, and countries. And it has the benefit of having been tested in a number of companies over the years. Implemented with integrity, it can provide that rare commodity that suppliers seek: superior business performance through demonstrating and documenting superior value.

TWO

Conceptualize Value

Focusing on What Matters

I N RECENT YEARS, the terms *value* and *value proposition* have become two of the most widely used terms in business markets. While these terms are fundamental to our customer value management approach, our research reveals that despite their growing use, there is little specificity or agreement about (1) what is value, (2) what constitutes a customer value proposition, and (3) what makes a value proposition persuasive.

Moreover, we find that most value propositions that suppliers construct and deliver in business markets do not actually convey the superior value their offerings may provide to customers. Lacking the knowledge to persuasively substantiate the superior value of their offerings relative to those offered by competitors, suppliers find that their value propositions are discounted by customer managers who, increasingly pressed for time and demonstrable results, focus simply on reducing price.

What *is* customer value in business markets? Offerings in business markets can have many value elements. How can identifying the points of difference, parity, and contention with the next-best alternative help firms focus on the relative handful that matter the most? What are the three alternative kinds of value propositions in practice, and which is best for suppliers to pursue? We answer each of these questions in turn—a solid grasp of these concepts is vital for moving business customers beyond price to demonstrated and documented superior value.

Defining Customer Value in Business Markets

What is meant, specifically, by "customer value in business markets"? We first consider how customer value has been defined by others and then focus on a superior definition. Next, we introduce the fundamental value equation to precisely express the relationship between customer value and price. We finish by discussing the customer's knowledge of value.

Conceptualizing Customer Value in Business Markets

Various definitions of *customer value* have been offered by different authors. Considering them suggests the varying conceptualizations underlying this concept and the differences in what it means. The definitions also suggest some of the difficulties in actually assessing customer value.[1]

According to Bradley Gale, "*Customer value* is market-perceived quality adjusted for the relative price of your product." Perhaps reflecting their interest in pricing, Robert Dolan and Hermann Simon state that "perceived value is the maximum price the customer will pay." Gerald Smith contends that "Value = the benefits the customer receives relative to the price paid." Finally, Thomas Nagle and Reed Holden state, "In common usage, the term *value* refers to the total savings or satisfaction that the customer receives from the product."[2]

So, what is customer value? Adjusted market-perceived quality, maximum price, benefits relative to price, totals savings, or, even, satisfaction received? Each of these constituent components takes our understanding of the concept in a different direction. Given that customers are happier paying a lower price, there appears to be tension between customer value as maximum price or satisfaction received. Yet the individuals providing these definitions do not go into much detail about what their definition means, nor do they discuss the conceptualizations of customer value that their definitions suggest.

Another problematic aspect about customer value that has not been addressed is how disparate constituent elements defining value might be combined. As an instance of this, consider benefits mentioned in the preceding definition from Smith. To make this tangible, consider two benefits for titanium dioxide, which is a pigment that whitens, brightens, and opacifies (as an ingredient in coatings). Each benefit is an improvement over a previous industry standard. Dispersability improves by reducing (from thirty minutes to ten minutes) the time required to reach 7 Hegman fineness units in a Cowles high-speed disperser. The second benefit, gloss, improves from 78 to 86 60° gloss units. How, specifically, a customer manager would combine Hegman fineness units and 60° gloss units is not at all clear. This example is typical of business markets where benefits—desirable changes in performance—are expressed in precisely defined scientific, engineering, and cost-accounting terms.

We find a number of elements in definitions of customer value: benefits, benefits expressed in monetary terms, costs, costs expressed in monetary terms, and price. What is lacking is a consideration of the commensurability of measurement units, which is essential to arrive at a meaning for customer value. Just as when one learns to combine fractions in school, one must first find a common denominator, convert the respective numerators to their units on this common denominator, and then combine them to reach an answer. So it would appear to be necessary in conceptualizing customer value, too. Of the five elements just given, however, only three have direct commensurability: benefits expressed in monetary terms, costs expressed in monetary terms, and price.

Conceptualizing Customer Value to Guide
Its Assessment in Practice

With its emphasis on assessing customer value in practice, customer value management requires a conceptualization of customer value that is well reasoned, comprehensive, and easily grasped. We start by defining customer value: "*Value in business markets* is the worth in monetary terms of the technical, economic, service, and social benefits a customer firm receives in exchange for the price it pays for a market offering."[3] We elaborate next on some aspects of this definition.

First, we express value in monetary terms, such as dollars per unit, euros per liter, or renminbi per hour. Economists may care about "utils," but we have never met a manager who did!

Second, we can conceptually represent any market offering as a set of economic, technical, service, and social benefits that a customer firm receives. By "benefits," we mean net benefits, which include any costs a customer incurs in obtaining the desired benefits, except for purchase price.

Third, value is what a customer firm gets in exchange for the price it pays. Raising or lowering the price does not change the set of benefits that an offering delivers to customers, only the willingness of those customers to purchase the offering. Thus, we conceptually view a market offering as having two elemental characteristics: its value and its price. That we do not include price as part of customer value is a critical distinction between our conceptualization and many others. To us, having price as a part of value adds considerable confusion. If we were to include price, we could significantly improve the value of our offering simply by cutting price dramatically, which goes against what most suppliers have in mind when they think of improving the value of their offerings to customers. It also goes against the fundamental concept of exchange in markets, where customers exchange money (i.e., price) with suppliers for offerings that the customers value.[4]

Finally, we contend that customer value in business markets is a comparative concept in which customers assess the value of a given market offering relative to what they regard as the next-best alternative to it. There *always* is an alternative. It might be:

1. A market offering from a competitor using comparable, or alternative, technology to fulfill the customer's requirements and preferences. This is the most frequently encountered situation in business markets.

2. The customer's decision to source an item from an outside supplier or to make the item itself. An example is a company that decides to outsource a part of its IT operations to an Indian supplier.

3. The status quo (i.e., not doing anything). Companies deciding whether to expand their facilities or purchasing management consulting services are examples.

4. The most recent offering from the same supplier. A challenge that Microsoft had, for example, was persuading its customers to upgrade from its Windows NT/2000 Server to its Windows XP Server when many of them still were satisfied with the performance of NT/2000 Server.

The Fundamental Value Equation

We can capture the essence of the concepts in our definition of value in a fundamental value equation:

$$(\text{Value}_f - \text{Price}_f) > (\text{Value}_a - \text{Price}_a) \quad (\text{Eq. 2-1})$$

In this equation, Value_f and Price_f are the value and price of a particular firm's market offering, and Value_a and Price_a are the value and price of the next-best-alternative market offering. In this fundamental value equation, we subtract price from value, relating them to one another in a difference formulation. We demonstrate the superiority of this formulation over a ratio formulation to interested readers in appendix A.

We do not specify a particular perspective in our definition of value, such as the customer firm's point of view, because we regard value in business markets as a construct, similar to market share. Because it is a construct, in practice, we can only estimate value, just as we can only estimate market share. For example, the supplier may overestimate the value of a given market offering to a customer, while the customer may underestimate the value. The supplier may have a significantly different perception than the customer of the technical, economic, service, and social benefits that the customer firm actually receives from a market offering or of what specific benefits are actually worth in monetary terms to the customer.

Value changes occur in two fundamental ways. First, a market offering could provide the same functionality or performance while its cost to the customer changes. Remember, price is not considered in this cost. Thus, the technical, service, and social benefits remain constant while the economic benefits change. For example, one product has higher value than another product because it has lower conversion costs and has the same performance specifications.

Second, value changes whenever the functionality or performance provided changes while cost remains the same (again, price is not a part of this cost). For example, a redesigned component part now provides longer usage until failure for the customer's customers, yet its acquisition and conversion costs to the customer remain the same.

Even if functionality or performance of a product is lowered, it may still meet, or even exceed, a customer's specified minimum requirement. More is better for some, but not all, customer requirements. Exceeding minimum requirements continues to deliver benefits to the customer, even though the customer deems a lesser level to be acceptable. For example, lowering the melting point of a plastic resin beyond a specified temperature requirement continues to lower the customer's energy costs and to reduce the time it takes to convert the resin into a molded plastic part.

In our definition value is the expression in monetary terms of what the customer firm receives in exchange for the price it pays for a market offering. Because make-versus-buy decisions are possible in business markets, the value provided must exceed the price paid. This difference between value and price is the *customer incentive to purchase*. Remember, in this concept of value in business markets, raising or lowering the price of an offering does not change the value that offering provides to a customer firm. Rather, it changes the customer's incentive to purchase that offering.

Having an accurate assessment of value provides a solid foundation for suppliers to create and deliver value to targeted market segments and customers. And recognizing that the value of a given market offering can vary by segment and by customer characteristics is vital. Suppliers practicing customer value management strive to both understand and capitalize on such variations.

The Customer's Knowledge of Value

In acquiring products and services, customer managers must decide which suppliers' market offerings will fulfill a set of requirements and preferences. When more than one supplier's market offering successfully fulfills these, customer managers then must decide which supplier's offering will deliver the greatest value to their firm. In many instances customer managers make this decision intuitively, simply choosing the offering that they feel is best (or, alternatively, that has the lowest price). Little or no effort is given to specifically defining what each manager means by "value" and how it might be estimated in monetary terms. As an example, customer managers may feel that it is not worthwhile to conduct a formal value assessment to acquire repositionable sticky notes and instead simply purchase 3M Post-it Notes, even if the price for them is slightly higher than lesser-known or generic brands.

In other instances, though, customer managers consider it worthwhile to conduct a formal assessment, or *value analysis*, to make a better informed decision. Progressive suppliers may assist customer managers in these assessments or even provide their own assessments of how their offerings deliver superior customer value. Customer value management focuses on these latter instances, where conceptualizing what exactly is meant by "value" and how to estimate it in practice are of principal interest.[5]

Customer firms often do not have an accurate understanding of what suppliers' market offerings actually are worth to them. Certainly, customers may understand their own requirements, but they do not necessarily know what fulfilling these requirements is worth to them, how differing ways of meeting these requirements affect their costs, or what changes in these requirements would be worth to them. As an example, Grainger tells its customers that acquisition costs often exceed the price of an item, particularly in the case of maintenance, repair, and operating supplies. We present a Grainger advertisement in figure 2-1 that illustrates this persuasively.

Points of Difference, Parity, and Contention

While the market offering of a supplier may deliver cost savings or incremental revenue and profit to customers in a number of ways, so, too, may the next-best alternative. Thus, although offerings in business markets may have many technical, economic, service, or social benefits that deliver value to customers, the paramount, overriding distinction to understand is this: how do these value elements compare to those of the next-best alternative? There are three possibilities:

1. *Points of parity*—those value elements whose performance or functionality is essentially the same as the counterpart elements of the next-best alternative

2. *Points of difference*—those value elements on which either the supplier's market offering is superior to those of the next-best alternative or the next-best alternative's market offering is superior to the supplier's

FIGURE 2-1

Grainger advertisement: Acquisition cost transcends price

We can help lower the costs of unplanned purchases.

Unplanned purchases are the purchases that you can't anticipate or predict in advance. When you add them all up, you spend more on unplanned purchases each year than you do on any other product category. In fact, the items you budget for in advance only account for about 60%* of your total purchases. And the more suppliers you're calling to cover those unplanned purchases, the more it costs your business.

Spend less time searching and more time on your business.
We specialize in the unplanned purchase because we can provide more products in more categories than ever before. If something unexpectedly breaks down or an emergency arises, make Grainger your first call. You stand a better chance of getting what you need right away than you do anywhere else. You'll spend less time looking for what you need, allowing you more time to focus on keeping your business running smoothly.

Don't overbuy. Make Grainger your inventory partner.
Once you've tracked down that hard-to-find item, it's very easy to overbuy in order to avoid the same lengthy process in the future. But when you buy more than you need, you have to store those items. And if they sit on the shelf too long, they can become obsolete, or expire. This all comes with a cost. Do yourself a favor and only buy what you need. Let us inventory the rest.

* *Source: Grainger Consulting Services*

GRAINGER
FOR THE ONES WHO GET IT DONE

Source: W. W. Grainger, Inc. Used with permission.

3. *Points of contention*—those value elements on which the supplier and its customers disagree about performance or functionality relative to the counterpart elements of the next-best alternative

Points of contention arise in two ways: the supplier regards a value element as a point of difference in its favor, while the customer regards that element as a point of parity relative to the next-best alternative; or the supplier regards a value element as a point of parity, while the customer regards it as a point of difference in favor of the next-best alternative.

Without getting too philosophical, we do not believe that there are multiple realities. We believe that there is only one reality but that the supplier and customer can have different perceptions of it. Far from being negative, points of contention provide motivation for the supplier and its customers to work together to gather data to resolve the differences in perception.[6]

The Three Kinds of Customer Value Propositions

Points of parity, points of difference, and points of contention are the inputs for developing the supplier firm's value proposition to the customer. When supplier managers use the term "customer value proposition," what specific meaning do they have in mind, and is this the same meaning that others have for this term? We have found in our research that there is considerable variation in what managers mean in their usage of "customer value proposition."[7]

From our research we can classify the substantially different ways managers use *customer value proposition* into three basic alternatives. We provide these alternatives in table 2-1 and organize our exposition of them to address four fundamental questions that distinguish the alternatives from one another:

TABLE 2–1

Value propositions in business markets: Which alternative conveys value?

	All benefits	Favorable points of difference	Resonating focus
Value proposition consists of:	All benefits customers receive from a market offering	All favorable points of difference a market offering has relative to the next-best alternative	The one or two points of difference (and, perhaps, a point of parity) whose improvement will deliver the greatest customer value for the foreseeable future
Value proposition answers this customer question:	"Why should our firm purchase your offering?"	"Why should our firm purchase your offering instead of your competitor's?"	"What is *most* worthwhile for our firm to keep in mind about your offering?"
Value proposition requires:	Knowledge of own market offering	Knowledge of own market offering and next-best alternative	Knowledge of how own market offering specifically delivers superior value to customers compared to next-best alternative
Value proposition's potential pitfall:	Benefit assertion	Value presumption	Requires customer value research

1. What does the value proposition consist of?

2. What customer question is the supplier attempting to answer with the value proposition?

3. What is required for a supplier to construct the value proposition and for the sales force to deliver it?

4. What is a potential pitfall of the value proposition?

All Benefits

The all-benefits customer value proposition is the meaning that supplier managers most frequently attach to the term. Why? It requires the least detailed knowledge about customers and competitors and, thus, is the easiest for supplier managers to construct and deliver. They simply list all the potential benefits they believe that their offering might deliver to targeted customers. The more they can think of, the better.

Yet simply listing all the benefits has the potential pitfall of *benefit assertion*: claiming distinctions for the offering that actually have no benefit to target customers. Consider the following example: a value-added reseller of gas chromatographs was accustomed to selling high-performance instruments to R&D laboratories in large companies, universities, and government agencies in Belgium, the Netherlands, and Luxembourg. One feature of a particular chromatograph, a patented injection system, enabled R&D lab customers to maintain sample integrity by avoiding high-temperature vaporization, eliminating the risk of thermal degradation, enhancing test discrimination, and permitting the use of volatile solvents. Seeking growth, the firm began to market the most basic model of this chromatograph to a new market (application) segment for the firm: contract laboratories.

In initial meetings with prospective contract lab customers, the firm's salespeople touted the injection system feature and its benefit of maintaining sample integrity. The prospects scoffed at this, stating that they were doing routine testing of soil and water samples for environmental regulation compliance, for which maintaining sample integrity was not a concern, and that room-temperature sample injection served their requirements adequately. The supplier was taken aback and forced to rethink its value proposition.

Another pitfall of the all-benefits proposition is that many, if not most, of the benefits may be points of parity with the next-best alternative, diminishing the effect of the few actual points of difference. An international engineering consulting firm was bidding for a light-rail project, and on the last chart of its presentation to the prospective municipal client, it listed the ten reasons why the municipality should award it the project. The other two finalist firms, though, could make most of the same claims because they were points of parity. Put yourself, for a moment, in the place of the prospective client. Suppose each firm, at the end of its presentation, gives ten reasons why you ought to award it the project. The lists are almost the same. How do you resolve the impasse? By asking each of the firms to "sharpen their pencils" and give a final best price. You then award the project to the firm that gives the largest price concession. Any distinctiveness that does exist between firms has been overshadowed by the greater overlapping sameness.

Favorable Points of Difference

The second customer value proposition, favorable points of difference, explicitly recognizes there is an alternative open to the customer. The recent experience of a leading industrial gas supplier underscores this distinction. It received a request for proposal from a customer for a major piece of business stating that the two or three suppliers that could demonstrate the most persuasive value propositions in their proposals would be invited to visit the supplier and to discuss and refine their proposals. After the meeting, the customer would select a supplier for this business.

As this example illustrates, "Why should our firm purchase your offering instead of your competitor's?" is a more pertinent question than "Why should our firm purchase your offering?" Why? Because the former question focuses supplier managers on differentiating their offering from the next-best alternative, which requires more detailed knowledge of it. A characteristic that the favorable-points-of-difference proposition shares with the all-benefits proposition, though, is that more is regarded as better, so supplier managers strive to list as many favorable points of difference as they can.

Knowing that an offering element is a point of difference relative to the next-best alternative does not, however, convey what the value of this difference is to target customers. Further, a supplier's market offering may have several points of difference relative to the next-best alternative, which complicates understanding which of them delivers the greatest value to target customers. Without a detailed understanding of the customer's requirements and preferences, and what it is worth to fulfill them, suppliers may stress points of difference that deliver relatively little value to the target customer. Each of these can lead to the potential pitfall of *value presumption*: assuming that favorable points of difference must be valuable for the customer. Our opening anecdote in chapter 1 about the IC supplier that unnecessarily discounted its price nicely illustrates the likely outcome when supplier salespeople stress favorable points of difference that actually have little value for the customer.

Resonating Focus

Although we contend that a favorable-points-of-difference proposition is preferable to an all-benefits proposition, we further contend that the third customer value proposition alternative, resonating focus, is the most preferred. We will go even further: the resonating-focus value proposition should be the gold standard for judging customer value propositions.

In a business world where customer managers are taking on greater responsibility and are increasingly pressed for time, to be successful, suppliers must deliver customer value propositions that are simple, yet powerfully captivating. They do this by making their offerings superior on the few elements whose functionality or performance matter most to target customers, by demonstrating and documenting the value of this superior performance, and by communicating it to customer managers in a way that conveys that the supplier understands the customers' business concerns and priorities. The resonating-focus customer value proposition consists of the one or two points of difference, and perhaps a point of parity, that deliver the greatest value to target customers.

This proposition differs from the favorable-points-of-difference proposition in two significant respects. First, more is not better. Although a supplier's offering may possess other favorable points of difference relative to the next-best alternative, the resonating-focus proposition steadfastly concentrates on the one or two points of difference that deliver, and whose improvement will continue to deliver, the greatest value to target customers. To better leverage limited resources, a supplier might even cede to the next-best alternative previous favorable points of difference that customers value the least, so that the supplier can concentrate its resources on improving the one or two points of difference customers value most.

Second, the resonating-focus proposition may contain a point of parity. This occurs either when the point of parity is required for target customers even to consider the supplier's offering or when a point of contention, where the next-best alternative was thought to be superior but research reveals it is not, is resolved in the supplier's favor.

To give practical meaning to the resonating-focus value proposition, let's consider a few examples. Sonoco approached a large European customer, a maker of consumer packaged goods, about redesigning the packaging for one of its product lines. Sonoco believed that the customer would profit from updated packaging, and by proposing the initiative itself, the company reinforced its reputation as an innovator. Although the redesigned packaging provided six favorable points of difference relative to the next-best alternative, Sonoco chose to emphasize one point of parity and two points of difference in its resonating-focus value proposition.

Sonoco's value proposition to the customer was that the redesigned packaging would have the same price as the present packaging but deliver significantly greater manufacturing efficiency in the customer's fill lines through higher-speed closing and provide a distinctive look that consumers would find more appealing than the present packaging.

Sonoco chose to include a point of parity in its value proposition because, in this case, the customer would not even consider a packaging redesign if the price were to increase. The first point of difference in the value proposition delivered cost savings to the customer, allowing it to move from a seven-day, three-shift production schedule during peak times to a two-shift, five-day operation. The second point of difference in the value proposition delivered an advantage at the consumer level, helping the customer incrementally grow its revenues and profits. In persuading the customer to change to the redesigned packaging, Sonoco did not neglect to mention the other favorable points of difference. Rather, it chose to place much greater emphasis on the one point of parity and the two points of difference that mattered most to the customer, thereby delivering a value proposition with resonating focus.

Stressing as a point of parity what customers mistakenly presume to be a point of difference favoring a competitor's offering can be an essential part of constructing a customer value proposition that has a resonating focus. Take the case of Intergraph, a provider of engineering software to engineering, procurement, and constructions firms—such as Fluor and Bechtel, which design, construct, and deliver process plants for their petrochemical, pharmaceutical, and power industry customers. One software product that Intergraph offers in its SmartPlant Engineering Solution is SmartPlant P&ID, which enables customers to define the flow processes (i.e., through valves, pumps, and piping) within plants they are designing and to generate piping and instrumentation diagrams (P&ID). Intergraph's resonating-focus value proposition for SmartPlant P&ID consists of one point of parity followed by three points of difference:

- Using SmartPlant, customers can create the P&ID graphics (i.e., drawings or reports) as fast, if not faster, than the next-best alternative.

- SmartPlant P&ID checks all the customer's upstream and downstream data related to plant assets and procedures— using universally accepted engineering practices, company-specific rules, and project- or process-specific rules—at each stage of the design process so that the customer avoids costly mistakes, such as reiterating the design or, worse, ordering the wrong equipment.

- SmartPlant is integrated with upstream and downstream tasks, such as process simulation and instrumentation design, thus requiring no reentry of data (and possible errors).

- With SmartPlant, the customer is able to link remote offices to execute the project and then merge the pieces into a single deliverable database to hand to its customer, the facility owner.

Intergraph has found it necessary to include the point of parity in its value proposition because some prospective customers wrongly presume that SmartPlant's drafting and graphic drawing performance is not as good as that of the next-best alternative. This presumption sometimes occurs because the next-best alternative is built on a computer-aided-design platform, whereas SmartPlant is built on a relational database platform. To counter this misperception, Intergraph has gathered data at reference customers to substantiate that this point of contention is actually a point of parity.

Resonating-focus value propositions have the potential pitfall of requiring customer value research. We find that customer value research is something that most suppliers, despite all the talk about customer value, have not actually done in a systematic way. Customer value research is not easy; it requires time, effort, persistence, and some creativity. Yet, as the experience of a leading resin supplier amply illustrates in chapter 4, *not* doing customer value research may actually be a greater pitfall.

Customer Value Propositions and Superior Business Performance

Constructing value propositions that resonate with target customers and substantiating them with customer value research enables

suppliers to achieve superior business performance. Let us provide a proof point for this. Consider the results for Intergraph. It
has posted revenue growth of 35 percent per year versus 10–12
percent for its industry. And, with today's emphasis on profitable
growth, Intergraph has a profit margin of 26 percent versus 14–16
percent for the industry.

Some managers, though, simply view value propositions as
something that the marketing folks do as a basis for creating business marketing communications such as advertising or signage for
trade show booths. We believe that this view is shortsighted and
neglects the potential contribution of value propositions to superior business performance. Properly constructed, customer value
propositions force companies to rigorously focus on their target
customer's requirements and preferences and what it is worth in
monetary terms to fulfill them. By involving managers from all
the relevant functional areas in the process, at least to some extent, the creation and assessment of value propositions provide a
means of forging shared understanding of what the supplier is
seeking to accomplish in the marketplace.

Viewed in this way, the value proposition statement can serve
as a guiding beacon and touchstone for the agreed-on market
strategy and, especially, as the answer to this question: "What do
we want to accomplish?" It puts into sharper focus which firms
the supplier regards as the relatively important customers, what
the supplier wants to emphasize about its market offering, and
what promise the supplier is making to customers about the value
they will receive. Everyone in the supplier's workforce needs to
have a good grasp on these issues.

Yet not everyone in the firm may want the greater direction
and focus that value proposition statements provide. For example, some may want to avoid value proposition statements, or to
write only vague ones, because they are afraid that customers
might find out that the supplier does not consider them the targets for an offering. These suppliers would rather have the customers, and their own sales force, believe that all customers are

equally good prospects for an offering! This not only dilutes the sales force's efforts and diminishes its motivation but can have further negative consequences when customers purchase an offering that was not designed to meet their requirements.

The resonating-focus value proposition for a market offering serves as the cornerstone for brand building in business markets. Although a number of points of difference and points of contention may have positive value estimates, we counsel suppliers to highlight in their resonating-focus value propositions the one or two that have the most value to target customer firms. Brand building for a market offering would then include devoting resources to significantly improve functionality or performance on those elements, demonstrating and documenting success in such improvements with customer value management, and persuasively communicating this progress to target customers.

Over time, customer value propositions can function as a reference standard in making decisions about contemplated changes in the market offering. Are the changes congruent and reinforcing, or will they subtly shift the character of the market offering? Either may be desirable, but by actively managing change, firms can avoid blurring their positioning in the marketplace. Thus, for example, the general manager of a business unit should be able to rely on a value proposition to guide decisions among conflicting tugs and pulls within the organization on how to further develop a market offering. In doing so, she focuses scarce resources on making the offering outstanding on the few elements that targeted customers value most and would be willing to reward the supplier for providing.

THREE

Formulate Value Propositions

Identifying Potentially Valuable Points of Difference

In the previous chapter, we emphasized that, to attain superior business performance, it is crucial for suppliers to develop a resonating-focus value proposition. In this chapter we describe a process for firms in business markets to formulate such a proposition. The process begins with the supplier hypothesizing present and potential points of difference to study that it believes are, or would be, valuable to target customers. The supplier may then conduct qualitative research to further refine the potential value proposition. Finally, it constructs value word equations to precisely express each point of difference and point of contention that it will estimate in the subsequent customer value research.

Hypothesize Present and Potential Valuable Points of Difference

Suppliers vary tremendously in their knowledge of how their offerings deliver value to target customers relative to the next-best-alternative offering. While some suppliers may have rigorously thought through this, most suppliers have only a sketchy and piecemeal understanding of their offering's value relative to the next-best alternative. So, to ascertain what the likely valuable points of difference are, a supplier most often begins by gathering what it knows about its offering relative to the next-best alternative for the target market. The outcome of this may be that the supplier identifies a few likely favorable points of difference (as well as any points of difference favoring the next-best alternative). Or the supplier may conclude that there are no discernable points of difference and that its offering is pretty much a commodity relative to the next-best alternative. In either case, because of the tremendous opportunity to learn in the customer value research, we advise suppliers to identify some prospective valuable points of difference to study. These may be changes in the market offering that the supplier already is planning to make in the near future (e.g., introducing a product enhancement or a new supplementary service). Alternatively, these may be prospective changes that the supplier could make in a reasonable period of time with reasonable investment *if* they were found to be sufficiently valuable to target customers.

Ascertain Present Points of Difference That Are Likely Valuable

To ascertain the present points of difference that are likely valuable to target customers, a supplier team (consisting of individuals from various functional areas who are knowledgeable about the offering and target customers) lists the value elements of the offering for the target market, decides which offering customers would regard as the next-best alternative, and evaluates its offering relative to that next-best alternative.

List the value elements. Offerings in business markets can have many value elements. Thus, it is best to list them quickly after the team selects the target market segment of interest. (Keep in mind that customer value proposition is a segment-specific notion.) Supplier teams tend to find this task easier when they first list out the value elements for the core product or service and then list the value elements for the augmenting services, programs, and systems that their company provides with its core product or service. Alternatively, the team could proceed by listing the value elements, in turn, that capture the technical, economic, service, and social benefits target customers receive from the offering, but teams tend to have more difficulty doing this.

It is fundamental that supplier teams be comprehensive and elemental in listing the offering's value elements. Leaving out elements, particularly ones that are unfavorable relative to the next-best alternative, compromises the effort and undermines its credibility with customers that detect the missing elements. By being as elemental as possible, the supplier firm is able to more accurately gauge the differences in functionality and performance its offering provides. For example, "provision of technical service" is simply too broad to enable a supplier to understand specifically how this element reduces customer costs or to compare its service's performance on this element to the next-best alternative. "Testing of customer samples" may be one constituent element of "provision of technical service," while "on-site equipment calibration" may be another. Furthermore, in subsequent customer value research, customer managers may find it easier to answer broadly stated questions, such as the cost of an hour of downtime in the customer's plant. However, their answers often will leave out effects on the customer's business processes (e.g., maintenance costs, disposal costs), producing less-valid estimates of worth.

Decide on the next-best alternative. Once the list of value elements is generated, the supplier next considers what would be the next-best alternative in the minds of target customers. Most often, this is the offering of the firm that most customers consider to be the supplier's principal competitor. However, as noted in the previous chapter, the next-best alternative may be the firm's own previous offering.

Usually, it is best to select one next-best alternative against which the firm's offering will be evaluated. However, on rare occasions, firms may choose to study two. This may be the case when the next-best alternative varies across country markets. For example, a supplier of medical diagnostic instruments may select one competitor's instrument as the next-best alternative in all the country markets of Europe, with the exception of Germany, where customers may regard a domestic competitor's instrument as the next-best alternative. In this instance, the firm would revisit its list of value elements, now making comparisons with this second alternative in mind.

Compare the firm's offering with the next-best alternative. While firms may be doing many wonderful things for their customers, the reality in most business markets is that so, too, are the competitors supplying the next-best alternative. So, to focus the subsequent customer value research and to make it more manageable, we've rearranged the fundamental value equation from chapter 2:

$$(\text{Value}_f - \text{Price}_f) > (\text{Value}_a - \text{Price}_a) \quad \text{(Eq. 3-1)}$$

$$(\text{Value}_f - \text{Value}_a) > (\text{Price}_f - \text{Price}_a) \quad \text{(Eq. 3-2)}$$

$$\Delta \text{Value}_{f,\,a} > (\text{Price}_f - \text{Price}_a) \quad \text{(Eq. 3-3)}$$

where:

Value_f = Value of the focal firm's market offering (Offering_f)

Price$_f$ = Price of the focal firm's market offering
(Offering$_f$)

Value$_a$ = Value of the next-best alternative's market offering
(Offering$_a$)

Price$_a$ = Price of the next-best alternative's market offering
(Offering$_a$)

Δ denotes the difference in value between Offering$_f$
and Offering$_a$

Thus, what really matters is not the value of each offering but the *difference* in value between the two offerings relative to the *difference* in their prices. Revisiting the list with this next-best alternative in mind, the team decides whether its offering's functionality or performance on each value element is comparable (i.e., a point of parity) or different (i.e., a point of difference) from that of the next-best alternative. We encourage teams to be candid in their appraisals.

Being elemental in the process also helps illuminate differences that would otherwise be lost. If you consider "technical service" as an element, well, almost every firm offers technical service; it is hardly a differentiator. If you are being elemental, you can ask several questions with respect to technical service to tease out the differences: How quickly does the firm answer a customer query compared to its competitor? What percentage of the time is the problem resolved with a single phone call? What percentage of the time is the problem resolved to the customer's satisfaction within one day?

If the team is honest with itself, it will pare down a lengthy list to only a handful of value elements that are differences between offerings. Most of these differences will be in favor of the team's offering, yet some will be differences favoring the next-best alternative. Teams typically believe that they have more favorable points of difference than they actually do. They tend to correctly identify the points of difference that receive positive estimates in the subsequent customer value research, but often one or more of these hypothesized points of difference turn out to be points of parity. The team later shares its thinking about points of parity and points of difference with those customers it invites to participate in the customer value research. In doing so, the team then surfaces the points of contention—the points of parity and points of difference on which it and the customers disagree.

Identify Prospective Changes to Create Superior Value

Customer value research gives a supplier a tremendous opportunity to learn how changes in its offering would increase the value relative to that of the next-best alternative. It is a chance to generate new knowledge for itself and the customers that participate in the research about which potential near-term changes in the offering would deliver the greatest incremental value. This provides terrific guidance to the supplier on how to allocate its scarce resources in ways that target customers would value most.

Yet suppliers frequently struggle to identify what potential changes would be worthwhile to study. The changes in the offering that they readily think of tend to be uninspired straight-line extensions of what they are currently doing. While this kind of thinking can surface some worthwhile changes, we encourage suppliers to stretch a little more and to include one or two potential changes that exhibit more creativity—something that many suppliers in business markets find challenging to do!

To generate some creative ideas that might substantially improve an offering's value to customers, consider the set of questions that Professors Chan Kim and Renée Mauborgne offer to promote out-of-the-box thinking. Specifically, supplier managers, salespeople, and field technical representatives should be asked to answer the following four questions with respect to the present offering or the existing value proposition.

1. *Reduce:* Which value elements should be reduced well below the industry standard?

2. *Raise:* Which value elements should be raised significantly above the industry standard?

3. *Eliminate:* Which value elements that the industry has taken for granted should be eliminated?

4. *Create:* Which new value elements should be created that the industry has never offered?[1]

As an example of reducing value elements, Medco, the pharmacy benefits management company, works on behalf of its corporate customers and health maintenance organizations to conduct studies on the efficacy of different drugs and their generic equivalents. These studies enable Medco to select, on behalf of its customers, which drugs will be on its preapproved lists. These preapproved lists reduce the number of choices of drugs that a physician can prescribe, recommending lower-cost generic equivalents instead.

NetJets, a firm offering fractional ownership of corporate jets, furnishes an example of raising value elements. Compared to first-class travel on commercial airlines, NetJets allows executives to choose from five thousand different airports for point-to-point travel. Since most of these are small regional airports, a busy executive can fly from, and land at, a more easily accessible airport than would often be the case for commercial airlines.

As an example of eliminating value elements, Dell chose not to offer the traditional benefits associated with purchasing computers from retail outlets to its small corporate customers, which were willing to forgo these benefits for lower prices.

Bloomberg, the financial information supplier, provides a noteworthy example of creating value elements. To create value for its customers, its terminals were designed with two flat-panel monitors so that traders could work with multiple windows simultaneously. In addition, its keyboards were developed with dedicated keys for the more familiar financial concepts and integrated analytical capability, which enable traders to analyze information with the press of a button.[2]

Conduct Qualitative Research to Refine the Value Proposition

To this point, the thinking and decisions of the team members draw on their collective experience, which should be extensive, but still represent an internal company view of the marketplace. Suppliers may find it comforting and worthwhile to get some customer feedback before proceeding with the more rigorous customer value assessment, which we detail in the next chapter. Some quick, relatively inexpensive qualitative research can provide a check that companies have not "fallen in love" with certain performance parameters that they are expert in and have distinct capability in advancing but that may no longer deliver the incremental value the supplier wants to believe. There are two recommended qualitative approaches in business markets: focus groups and visiting customers.

Conduct Focus Groups

Focus groups are sessions in which a moderator exposes participants to potential product offerings or concepts and asks for their perceptions and reactions. Participants typically are knowledgeable individuals within customer firms that are targets for the studied market offering, although a supplier firm also may be interested in the reactions of industry consultants or pundits. The moderator might ask the participants to make rough trade-offs on which prospective changes they would find most valuable. In doing so, the analyst generates insights into what changes in the offering might be most valuable, potential subsegments, and op-

portunities for differentiation—in other words, grist for constructing potential resonating-focus value propositions.

Whenever possible, we advocate conducting these focus groups
during a customer industry event, such as a convention or trade
show. This facilitates getting customers to participate, because
they will be attending the event anyway, and lowers the cost of
getting a diverse group of customers together. We prefer to use the
term *business roundtable discussion* in place of *focus group* because the former sounds more interesting and inviting to prospective participants. It also better describes what we seek: an open
exchange between participants of how changes in supplier offerings would better fulfill customers' requirements and preferences.

Spend a Day in the Life of the Customer

A litmus test for customer value management is determining
whether new knowledge of how to add value and reduce cost has
been generated. In other words, have both the supplier and the
customers that participate in the customer value research each
gained a better understanding of how the supplier's offering can
add value or reduce cost in the customers' business? Although
focus groups are good at getting customer reaction to specific potential offerings, they require the supplier to already know what
those sources of value might be. When the supplier is seeking to
discover new potential sources of value, the "day in the life of the
customer" (DLC) approach is preferred.[3]

Axios Partners is a management consulting firm that focuses
on customer value management and assists its clients in conducting
DLC studies to generate insights into potential sources of customer value.[4] In DLC research Axios stresses the active participation of managers from various functions at the supplier as well as
at the customer. Each function views the world differently, and
that divergence of perspective increases the likelihood that new
knowledge and understanding will emerge from the research.
Axios also finds that on-site observation is superior for finding

new value or cost savings of which the customer is unaware. This research is more than just looking for frustrations that the customer can already articulate: the supplier team and the participating customer managers search for things that have been accepted as a given or never previously recognized as an opportunity to improve the way business is done. Consider two recent Axios client experiences with DLC research.

A supplier was exploring how to improve the design process for subsystems that industrial engineers at its customers—all original equipment manufacturers—used. The supplier had been publishing a parts catalog on CD-ROM for years, yet customer engineers reported that they never used it even though it was more up-to-date than the paper catalog. The engineers would say that they preferred the paper catalog, but they couldn't articulate why. While on a customer visit, the supplier research team had a design engineer go to his desk and walk through how he found a part for a new product. On his bookshelf he had not only the current catalog but also the previous two years of catalogs. They were filled with Post-it Notes and handwritten comments about specific parts. The CD-ROM didn't offer the engineer and his colleagues the ability to keep track of their personal experiences with the products. Based on this new knowledge, the supplier designed an online catalog in which users could save their personal comments about specific products for later review or reuse. This seemingly minor capability helped engineers better select the part for the application in less time. As a result, there was a significant increase in new customer products that specified the supplier's parts.

IKOR is an industry-leading provider of power management and conversion solutions for the computing marketplace. It recently conducted DLC research with workstation and server manufacturers to evaluate the opportunity for its innovative, recently patented technology. During these visits, which delved into various aspects of designing power for new systems' architectures, the IKOR research team discovered significant power-related problems with electronic systems integration that had largely been ignored. The silver box (SB) in workstations and servers is the unit that handles the initial AC-to-DC power conversion, and it contains its own internal fans to dissipate the significant amount of heat it generates. The team discovered that the SB design of the leading vendor was five years behind the technology needed to keep pace with even existing systems and was a limiting technology that forced trade-offs, such as those between footprint and noise (smaller boxes meant more-powerful fans running harder to manage heat dissipation). This insight led IKOR to enter this business with a totally redesigned SB that has increased efficiency, decreased heat loss, and increased airflow, allowing for slower fans and less noise without affecting the processor's performance. This innovative SB design is opening up a new world of configuration options for IKOR customers, enabling them to push the boundaries of systems design, with power no longer the accepted or expected limiting factor.

Construct Value Word Equations

Central to customer value management is expressing in monetary terms the worth of the technical, economic, service, and social benefits that a customer firm receives from a supplier's offering. Doing this in practice is not easy and takes time, money, persistence, and some creativity. Yet businesses must tackle this challenging task if they wish to become value merchants. As examples, consider the following:

- An economic benefit such as providing consolidated monthly invoices instead of invoicing the customer after each purchase must be translated into processing costs savings over the year for the customer.

- A technical benefit such as easier release from a diamond-like coating applied to plastic injection molds that results in fewer machine jams and faster operations must be translated into additional revenue and profit that the customer would generate from greater uptime and faster cycle time.

- A unique service such as a chemical supplier collecting used drums from the customer's site must be translated into the customer's cost savings from not having to dispose of used containers in an environmentally safe way.

- A social benefit such as Caterpillar's strong brand name must be translated into the higher resale or trade-in prices that Caterpillar equipment receives versus Komatsu, reducing its life-cycle cost to customers.

Unfortunately, most firms in business markets feel more comfortable presenting features and benefits to customers rather than the worth of those benefits to the customer in monetary terms. And, in any case, they are unsure about how to translate the differential benefits that their firm's offering has over the next-best alternative into monetary terms.

Value word equations are a tool that enables a supplier to demonstrate and document points of difference and points of contention for its offering relative to the next-best alternative so that customer managers can easily grasp them, understand precisely how the supplier is assessing them, and be persuaded by the results. Value word equations provide a methodical way of convincingly demonstrating and documenting superior value in monetary terms.

A *value word equation* expresses precisely in words and simple mathematical operators (e.g., +, ÷) how to assess the differences in functionality or performance between a supplier's offering and the next-best alternative on a value element and how to convert those differences into monetary terms. One is constructed for each point of difference (and point of contention). The value element, expressed as either cost savings or incremental profit, is on the left side of the equal sign, and the components defining the differences in functionality or performance and what they are worth are on the right side. Accompanying each word equation are the assumptions that the supplier is making about the value element and how its monetary value is assessed.

Value word equations counter two rampant problems in business markets. The first is *value claims*—that is, when suppliers argue that their offerings deliver cost savings or added value relative to the next-best alternative but can provide little or no specifics of exactly how this occurs. With each retelling, the value claims from these unverifiable stories tend to grow larger and larger, taking on the character of "fishing tales."

The second rampant problem is "spreadsheet mania": the construction of overly complicated, difficult-to-understand spreadsheets by technically minded individuals who want to show off their Excel skills. The result is densely packed, number-laden spreadsheets with minimal to nonexistent explanations of what the numbers mean. When questioned about the content of these spreadsheets, even their creators sometimes have difficulty reconstructing the numbers' meaning.

In contrast to this, firms such as Intergraph and Rockwell Automation use value word equations to make it clear and easily understandable to customers how their offerings will lower costs or add value relative to the next-best alternative, what data needs to be gathered, and how this data will be combined to provide value estimates. Intergraph uses a laptop tool to enable its sales representatives to do this. Frank Joop, who is responsible for business development for Intergraph's SmartPlant Engineering Solution, believes that his prospective customers, who are nearly all engineers (as he is), want to see the equations that define precisely how cost savings will occur. In our research interview, he observed, "As an engineer, I want to see the formula . . . How do you get to this number?"[5]

Accompanying each word equation are the assumptions that the team is making about the value element and how its monetary value is assessed. In all customer value research, some assumptions will be needed to complete the analysis. The assumptions might be about the functionality or performance the market offering actually provides in the customer's specific setting, particularly for aspects that are extraordinarily difficult or costly to measure. Alternatively, assumptions might be made in assigning worth in monetary terms to measured differences in the performance that an offering provides in the customer's setting.

It is crucial that the supplier be explicit in the assumptions it makes. When a customer firm catches the supplier in one or more implicit assumptions, particularly ones that are dubious, it can have a devastating effect on the credibility of the whole analysis. In contrast, when all assumptions are made explicit, customer management can simply disagree with them. When this happens, the astute supplier invites customer managers to share the rationales underlying their alternative assumptions. Depending on how plausible their rationales seem, the supplier can either adopt the alternative assumptions for the analysis or suggest that the supplier and customer engage in some joint research to mutually discover the most appropriate assumptions for the customer's specific setting.

The data for the value word equations is most often collected from the customer's business operations by supplier and customer managers working together, but at times, data may come from outside sources, such as industry association studies. In presentations of the results, each word equation is presented first. Then the data is substituted in each equation to calculate the estimate. These results are then collected in a value summary, which we refer to as the *customer value model*.

Value Word Equations at Rockwell Automation

Consider a value word equation that Rockwell Automation used to calculate the cost savings from reduced power usage that a customer would gain by using a Rockwell pump solution instead of a competitor's comparable offering:

Power reduction

cost savings = [kW spent • number of operating hours per year
         • $ per kW hour • number of years system
       solution in operation]$_{\text{Competitor Solution}}$ −

[kW spent • number of operating hours per year
• $ per kW hour • number of years system
solution in operation]_{Rockwell Solution}

The term *kW spent* represents the amount of electrical power consumed and is defined by the equation: kW spent = unit horsepower • 0.746 • 1/unit efficiency. Unit horsepower and unit efficiency are industry-standard product specifications that the manufacturer prominently displays on the side of the motor solution, and 0.746 is a standard electrical-engineering conversion factor that translates horsepower into units of electricity.

Although the meaning of this value word equation may seem obscure, it reflects the heavy usage of industry-specific jargon that suppliers and customers in business markets rely on to communicate precisely and efficiently about functionality and performance.

Value Word Equations at a Commercial Roofer

In some business markets—such as commercial roofing, management consulting, or commercial insurance—it is more difficult for customers to split their business between two or more suppliers. While business customers in these markets may consider the alternative offerings of competing suppliers, they tend to select a single supplier for their business. Thus, it is difficult to make actual comparisons of the performance of one supplier's offering with another supplier's offering when only one supplier will actually get the business. In these kinds of situations, the next-best alternative may be the expectations of the customers, based on their own past experiences or on the experiences of consultants they hire to advise them. Nonetheless, it is still worthwhile to construct value word equations, but in this case, they should capture the supplier's actual performance versus expected performance.

As an example, consider a recent experience of ours working with commercial roofing contractors. A commercial roofing contractor was competing with others for reroofing juice-processing plants in Florida. This contractor, which we will call ComRoof, was successful and won the business at a plant that was part of a large consumer products firm. As is increasingly common these days, this firm outsources the planning, design, and supervision of the major maintenance and reconstruction of its plants to an engineering consulting firm. This engineering consulting firm, which we will call Con, had established estimates, based on its experience, on the number of days it would take to complete the tasks in reroofing a juice-processing plant.

The old roofing and the insulation under it needed to be removed before the new insulation and roofing could be installed. While the old materials were being replaced, the plant would have elevated refrigeration costs to maintain the cool interior temperature, which is critical in juice processing. Through superior project management and on-site job supervision, ComRoof was able to complete this reroofing project considerably faster than Con had estimated. The following value word equation captures what fewer days of elevated refrigeration costs are worth:

Elevated refrigeration

cost savings = (Estimated elevated days$_{Con}$ – Actual elevated days$_{ComRoof}$) • elevated refrigeration electricity cost per day

Where:

Elevated refrigeration

electricity cost per day = Electricity cost per day for cooling during reroofing – Electricity cost per day for cooling before removing old roof

This case also affords us a chance to see how it is so important to be comprehensive and elemental. Might there also be other cost savings, under certain conditions, such as the frequent case when the new insulation and roofing have a higher R-factor (a measure of thermal resistance) than the previous insulation and roofing? We would capture the worth of this with the following value word equation:

Earlier higher *R*-factor

refrigeration cost savings = (Electricity cost for cooling per $\text{day}_{\text{old roof}}$ – Electricity cost for cooling per $\text{day}_{\text{new roof}}$) • Number of days reroofing completed ahead of estimate

ComRoof senior management, which had not previously thought about the superior value of their reroofing process in such a methodical way, agreed that it could readily obtain the data needed to estimate these value word equations. Armed with this knowledge, it would be in a much better position to demonstrate and document the value of its superior performance to present and prospective juice-processing plant customers.

For another example of using value word equations, see the PeopleFlo EnviroGear Pump customer value model in appendix B.

FOUR

Substantiate Value Propositions

Demonstrating and Documenting Superior Value

CUSTOMER MANAGERS in a series of business roundtable discussions we conducted in Europe and the United States related to us that prospective suppliers increasingly deliver to them what has become almost a generic value proposition: "We can save you money!" But, as one participant in Rotterdam wryly observed, with all the claims about how much money suppliers were saving him, it was a wonder that his firm had any costs left at all! To assess the validity of these claims, though, he said that he would follow up a prospective supplier's statement with a series of questions to probe whether the supplier had the people, process, tools, and experience to substantiate its claims. He recounted that based on their answers, most of the suppliers were telling fairy tales.

Simply put, to make customer value propositions persuasive, suppliers must be able to demonstrate and document them. Value word equations, which we discussed in the last chapter, provide a methodical way of precisely expressing differences between the supplier's offering and the next-best alternative and how those differences translate into monetary terms. These value word equations are brought alive, though, by gathering data in customer value research. Drawing on the insights gained in the customer value research for the customer value proposition, the supplier goes on to tailor market offerings to deliver superior value, which we will discuss in the next chapter. The supplier also creates tools to persuasively demonstrate and document that superior value, thus enabling it to substantiate its value proposition to target customers.

Conduct Customer Value Research

The supplier decides on the offering and the target market segments it will study in each customer value research project. The goal of this research is to generate new knowledge of how the offering adds value or reduces costs for customers relative to the next-best alternative. A related goal is to gain new knowledge of how this superior value varies across customers. This enables the supplier to better pinpoint the kinds of customers to target. Thus, in designing each research project, the supplier further segments, or subsegments, the market based on descriptors that it hypothesizes would lead customers to receive more value or less value from its offering relative to the next-best alternative. Most often, to keep the projects manageable, two segments or subsegments are selected for study, which provides a contrast for the supplier to test its hypothesis.[1]

The composition of each customer value research team will vary, depending on the nature of the project, but often includes someone who most often spends time at the customer solving problems (e.g., a field technical rep or field applications engineer); someone from the product marketing or development functional area; and two or three progressive salespersons. Having salespersons involved at the start is crucial. They provide needed expertise on the customer and its use of the offering, and they have knowledge of and relationships with customers that would be willing to cooperate in customer value research. Being part of a customer value management initiative from the outset also builds support for the approach with those salespeople, who then can persuasively relate their experiences to others in the sales force. Having these salespeople as internal champions is critical for transforming the sales force into value merchants, as we discuss in chapter 6.

Each team should have a leader selected by senior management before the start of the project. The team leader should be someone with superior project management and interpersonal skills. We recommend that the manager with primary responsibility for implementing the business case for change *not* be the team leader. For example, although the product manager for a new offering who has to decide which market segment to enter initially will be a significant contributor to the team, it is preferable to give a more objective manager the primary responsibility for the project management and process aspects of the team's work.

Customer value assessments are an intensive analytical effort, which may require up to a half-time commitment by the project leader. Other team members will spend varying amounts of time on the project, with a quarter-time commitment being typical. This time commitment fluctuates, though, with team members spending several days a week on the project at some points (e.g., field visits to customers participating in the research to gather data) but virtually no time on it at other points.

For customer value research projects to succeed, the active support of senior management is crucial. Most often, a senior manager acts as a sponsor for each team. This should be decided before the start of the projects. As we mentioned in chapter 1, while senior managers should communicate to the teams the importance of the pilot program to the business, they make a more visible statement through how they spend their own time. Making the commitment to attend at least the opening morning of the customer value work-shop, to monitor the progress of teams, and to attend the presentation day for the business cases sends a strong signal to the teams.

The customer value research proceeds in three phases: gaining initial customer cooperation, gathering the data, and analyzing the data. It concludes with constructing a business case for change, which charts out the customer value proposition that the business wants to realize with target customers. We finish this explanation of customer value research with a real-world case study.

Gain the Customer's Cooperation

Before contacting any present or prospective customers to participate in the research, the team has some tasks to perform. First, it must decide on the present or prospective customers that it wants to participate. Although the number of research participants will depend on the market, typically the team seeks to include six to eight customers from each segment.

The team next thinks through why the customers should cooperate in the research. We have found that a useful device for this is a *"gives & gets" analysis.* "Gives" capture the specific investments and resources that each firm is expected to contribute to the research, such as managers' time and data. "Gets" capture the specific gains that each firm expects to receive, such as research findings and cost-savings recommendations. We illustrate this analysis conceptually in figure 4-1.

The challenge for the team is to understand and evaluate the gives and gets from its firm's perspective *and* from the perspectives of the customer firms participating in the research. For example, does what the supplier perceives that it is giving correspond to what the customer perceives that it is getting, or is there some discrepancy? Moreover, team members need to discover gives that they can provide that would have more value to the customer than that customer's perception of its cost of the gives that it is being asked to provide to the supplier. In our experience cus-

FIGURE 4-1

"Gives & Gets" analysis

Evaluate:

1. Are supplier's "gives" the same as customer's "gets," and are supplier's "gets" the same as customer's "gives"?
2. Is customer's "gets" value > customer's "gives" cost? Is supplier's "gets" value > supplier's "gives" cost?
3. Is the customer's "gets" value > supplier's "gives" cost? Is supplier's "gets" value > customer's "gives" cost?

tomers cooperate in customer value research for one or more of four basic reasons: a low-cost resource to better understand their business, an opportunity to benchmark, earlier access to some new product or service, or get a meaningfully lower price. The team should decide on several increasing levels of incentives that it could offer customers, successively if needed, to gain their participation in the research.

The team next contacts the salesperson responsible for each customer, explains the purpose of research, and gains the salesperson's support. The salesperson provides names and contact information for customer managers to invite to the initial meeting, where those managers will learn the purpose of the research and be asked to cooperate. Depending on company protocol, the salesperson responsible for each customer may accompany the team members to the initial meeting. (It must be stressed, though, that this meeting is *not* a sales call.) And at least two team members should visit each customer whenever possible.

Gather Data

In the initial meeting, the team members explain the purpose of the research and what the customer can expect to gain from participating. Team members relate the list of value elements and which ones they regard as points of parity and points of difference. They can check for comprehensiveness by asking the customer managers whether any value element has been inadvertently left out that might be a point of difference. The team members then share the initial value word equations for the hypothesized points of difference.

If team members have been honest with themselves, the customers will largely agree with them. Inevitably, though, customers will disagree with the team's assessment on some value elements. For example, the customer might regard a point of parity as a point of difference favoring the next-best alternative. These disagreements determine the value elements that are points of contention. Such disagreements should not be regarded as problems because they provide further motivation to the customers to participate in research and gather data to resolve the points of contention.

Revisiting the points of difference and points of contention, the team members discuss what sources of data the customer presently generates, or would be able to generate, to provide an estimate of each point of difference and point of contention. They discuss timing and resource requirements for data collection. Finally, they discuss what sources of data outside the customer firm (e.g., industry association studies) might be worthwhile to pursue.

In doing the research, wherever possible, the team prefers to gather data rather than rely simply on customer perception. If the customer volunteers to generate or collect the data, the team should inquire into the method that will be used. How reliable will the measurement be? That is, how consistent will the measurements be over time, or are there variations that need to be considered? What assumptions are being made? Whenever possible, team members should offer to work with the customer to generate or gather the data. Depending on the situation, a second visit to the customer likely will be needed to do this.

The team needs to be creative, using other sources when desirable or necessary. Independent industry consultants or knowledgeable personnel within the supplier firm can be sources of initial estimates. In some instances retired customer personnel may be a resource. When the provision of a service element mitigates a risk the customer could otherwise encounter, supplier firms sometimes employ actuarial consultants to estimate the cost of that risk. Qualcomm drew on American Trucking Association research studies to provide ranges for some of the elements in its value model for its OmniTRACS mobile communication system.

Finally, the team members consider *value placeholders*, which are value elements that the supplier believes are worth something to customers but either are too difficult to obtain data for or are social elements. In such cases the team will have to rely on customer perception: What qualitatively is each value element worth, and how might proxy estimates be obtained? When there is no other source than customer perception, framing the worth of the element in the customer's mind to establish a reference point is critical.

Analyze the Data

When the data has been gathered, the team analyzes it to estimate what each point of difference or point of contention is worth in monetary terms. It also calculates the mean and the variance (or standard deviation) for each. It then conducts comparisons between the two studied segments to understand how the estimate for each value element varies across the two. The team next summarizes these results in the *customer value model*. The team should be certain to list any assumptions made in assigning monetary amounts to each element.

To gain a deeper understanding of the results, the team performs sensitivity analyses, using the information on the variances related to each element. It considers what characteristics might drive the variation in value and whether that variation warrants a new segmentation approach. It identifies which customers are the most attractive prospects.

The team finally considers the value placeholders. What insights can be provided? How should the value placeholders be used in light of the customer value assessment? Although Qualcomm assigns no monetary amounts to less tangible elements, it still includes them in its analysis as value placeholders. In this way, Qualcomm conveys that it believes those elements are worth something to the customer and leaves open the possibility that some specific amount might be ascertained in the future.

Construct a Business Case for Change

Based on the knowledge of value that the team has gained from its research, what does it recommend that the business do differently? What is the customer value proposition that will resonate with targeted customers? The business case for change should address:

1. What specific actions does the team recommend based on its customer value research?

2. What resources would be needed to accomplish the recommended changes in doing business?

3. What are the specific concerns in implementing the business case?

4. What milestones can be specified to chart the progress in accomplishing the change?

5. What would be the incremental profitability if the business case for change were approved?

Think of the business case for change as specifying what the business needs to do differently to enable it to realize a resonating-focus customer value proposition. This list may include developing the core product or service to strengthen its performance or provisioning new supplementary services valued by target customers. The business case for change may also specify upgrades in the sales force's capability—for example, to do the consultative selling required to understand customer requirements and preferences and to tailor the market offering to deliver superior value.

The team leaders present their business cases to senior managers who have served as project sponsors and to the top management of the business unit. Each business case should be viewed as a prospective commitment: if senior management provides the requested resources, the business will deliver the specified results, especially the estimated incremental profitability. After all, it does the business no good to make changes to deliver superior value if it does not get a fair return for doing so.

Transform a Weak Value Proposition into Resonating Focus

A leading supplier of resins to coatings producers for architectural applications—that is, paint for buildings—recognized that its customers were coming under pressure to reduce volatile organic compounds (VOCs) from coatings to comply with increasingly strict environmental regulations. (Resins are the backbone of a coating, composing 30–60 percent of a coating by volume.) Producers were pursuing either new formulations of coatings that significantly reduced solvents (the source of VOC emissions) or water-borne systems that contained minimal or no solvents—although both solutions resulted in a sacrifice in product performance.[2]

This resin supplier responded with a new type of resin that would enable its coatings customers to remain compliant with stricter environmental standards while retaining most of the desirable performance characteristics of solvent-based paints, albeit at a higher price. This resin supplier offered what it later came to realize was a linear, or single-dimensional, value proposition: "The new resin provides coatings producers with VOC compliance while retaining the performance of similar noncompliant resins at a somewhat higher price." In their initial discussions with targeted coatings customers that were testing the resin product, the resin supplier was surprised and disappointed at the tepid reaction it received, particularly from commercial managers at the customers. They were not enthusiastic about the sales prospects for higher-priced coatings containing the new resin with commercial painting contractors, the primary target market, and they indicated that they would not move to the new resin until regulation mandated it. The value proposition for the new resin was not persuasive, and potential for the new resin appeared limited, at best.

Taken aback by this, the resin supplier decided to broaden its focus and do customer value research to better understand the requirements and preferences of its customers' customers—commercial painting contractors—and how the performance of its resin would affect their total cost of doing business. The requirements and preferences of the commercial painting contractors' customers—building owners—were even studied. The resin supplier used a series of combined focus groups and field tests with painting contractors to gather data on three types of coatings: traditional solvent-based coatings, the advanced solvent-based coating that would be VOC compliant, and a water-borne coating. The performance on primary customer requirements—such as coverage, dry time, and durability—was studied. Customers were asked to make performance trade-offs and indicate their willingness to pay for coatings that deliver enhanced performance. The resin supplier also joined a commercial painting contractor industry association, took courses on how contractors are taught to estimate jobs, and learned to use the job estimation software painting contractors use in order to better understand the value proposition of the new product.

Several insights emerged from this customer value research. Only 15 percent of a painting contractor's costs are the coatings; labor is by far the largest cost component. This information indicated that if a coating provided greater painter productivity, an increased selling price might be accepted by contractors. Contractors value coatings that provide superior coverage (so that more can be applied with each stroke, thereby reducing the coats required for the same coverage) and have a faster dry time (four hours or less versus eight hours or more for conventional solvent-based paints) so that two coats can be applied during a single eight-hour shift.

The resin supplier was pleasantly surprised to discover that in addition to being VOC compliant, its new resin possessed properties that delivered superior value to its customers' customers, and with some minor tweaking, the new resin could deliver still more value. The new resin enabled a higher film build with a coating, providing better hiding power and coverage, and could provide a drying time that allowed recoating in less than four hours. The resin supplier retooled its value proposition from a single dimension—VOC compliance—to a resonating-focus value proposition in which VOC compliance was a relatively minor part. The new value proposition was this: "The new resin enables coatings producers to make architectural coatings providing higher film build and the ability to put on two coats within a single shift, thus increasing painter productivity while also being VOC compliant." Coatings customers enthusiastically accepted this value proposition, and the resin supplier was able to get a 40 percent price premium for its new offering over the traditional resin product.

Demonstrate Customer Value Through Value Calculators

Suppliers need to convince prospective customers beforehand what cost savings or added value they can expect from using the supplier's offering relative to the next-best alternative. Firms practicing a value-based approach to business markets, such as GE Infrastructure Water & Process Technologies and SKF, demonstrate the value of their offerings in advance through *value calculators*. These tools are spreadsheet software applications that salespeople or value specialists use on laptop computers, as part of a consultative selling approach, to demonstrate the value that customers likely would receive from the offerings.

Orange Orca B.V. is a management consulting firm, based in the Netherlands, that is committed to change management and measurable improvement of performance for its clients.[3] As part of this, it assists its clients in building value calculators to demonstrate the superior value of their offerings to target customers. To understand what value calculators look like, see figure 4-2, which presents an example of a summary screen—that is, a customer value model—and a screen corresponding to one of the points of difference for a client's new polymer (note: InnoPackaging and European Petrochemical Company are pseudonyms). Using this calculator, the client's salespersons were able to demonstrate the superior value the polymer delivered at similar customer firms and consequently gained more business at a higher price per ton for their company's Transplast polymer.

A recent experience from Rockwell Automation exemplifies how value calculators can provide supplier salespeople with a competitive edge.[4] A condiment producer hastily summoned a Rockwell Automation sales representative, Jeff Policicchio, to participate in a "continuous improvement conference" at one of its major plant sites. Facing considerable pressure from Wal-Mart to lower condiment prices, the producer decided to invite its incumbent suppliers as well as competing suppliers to a meeting designed to find ways to dramatically reduce its operating costs. Along with competing supplier sales reps, Policicchio was given full access to the plant and its personnel for one full day.

From discussions with plant personnel, Policicchio quickly learned that a major and recurring problem stemmed from lost production and downtime attributable to poorly performing pumps on thirty-two huge condiment storage tanks. Using Rockwell's TCO Toolbox, an interactive laptop software program (TCO stands for "total cost of ownership"), Policicchio generated a list of probing questions designed to gather data associated with pump usage. Through extensive interviews with the plant engineer, maintenance manager, and purchasing manager, Policicchio gathered relevant cost and usage data and entered it into his laptop's TCO Toolbox program. Based on an assessment of data, he was

FIGURE 4-2

Transplast value calculator: Summary screen

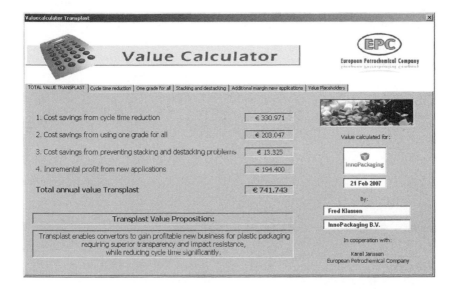

Transplast value calculator: Screen for calculating first value element

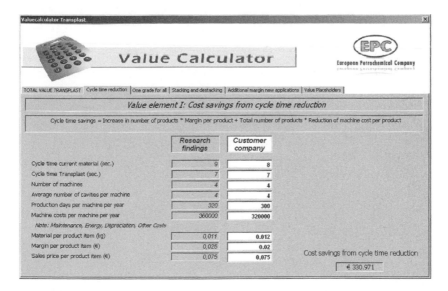

Source: Orange Orca B.V. Used with permission.

then able to construct a "pump solution," or what the trade calls a "screw-drive," composed of a Reliance Electric XE motor, a Dodge Quantis gear reducer, and a Reliance Electric variable-frequency drive.

The next day Policicchio and his competitors were called back to the plant and given one hour to prepare a solution proposal and present it to plant management. Again, Policicchio used his TCO Toolbox program to generate a value assessment report, craft a value proposition, and prepare a set of slides for his presentation. Following the presentations, Policicchio learned that he was the only one to use a value assessment tool to demonstrate tangible cost savings attributable to his proposed solution. Everyone else made fuzzy promises about possible benefits. Stated simply, Policicchio's value proposition was "Through this Rockwell Automation pump solution, your company will save at least $16,268 per pump (on up to thirty-two pumps) relative to our best competitor's solution through the elimination of most downtime, reduced administrative costs associated with procurement, and lower spending on repair parts."

Plant managers were so impressed with Policicchio's value proposition that they immediately purchased one pump solution for a trial examination. After a trial period, they audited its performance and discovered it to be even better than predicted. Based on these findings, they placed orders for the remaining pumps. These will be installed as the existing pumps wear out.

Demonstrate Customer Value Through Comparative Tests

When necessary, best-practice suppliers go to extraordinary lengths to demonstrate the comparative value of their offerings relative to the next-best alternative's. These suppliers realize that prospective customers find comparative tests powerfully persuasive. Rather than shy away from making explicit comparisons, such suppliers recognize that customers are going to make such evaluations anyway, so these suppliers take the initiative themselves. Consider the recent experiences of Akzo Nobel and Thales Nederland.

The polymer chemical unit of Akzo Nobel recently conducted a two-week pilot on a production reactor at a prospective customer to gather data firsthand on the performance of its high-purity metal organics (HPMO) offering relative to the next-best alternative in producing compound semiconductor wafers. Akzo Nobel paid this prospective customer for two weeks of time at its production reactor, where each day served as a separate trial because of daily considerations such as output and maintenance. Instead of hand-waving about the scaling of its Epiproof HPMO offering from an R&D reactor to a production reactor and making assumptions about the cost savings, Akzo Nobel now has real data from an actual production machine and tangible evidence that the wafer produced is as good as or better than the one the customer currently grows using the next-best alternative.

To let its prospective customers' customers (i.e., the firms making the wafers into compound semiconductors) verify this data for themselves, Akzo Nobel brought wafers it had produced to them for testing. Akzo Nobel combines this point of parity with two points of difference—significantly lower energy costs and maintenance costs—to provide a value proposition with a resonating focus.

Thales Nederland, on the other hand, is a leading contractor in providing defense electronics and radar systems to governments for their navies. At times, it will arrange comparative field tests to demonstrate the superior value of its offering relative to the next-best alternative. The Royal Dutch Navy, which is a well-equipped and provisioned client of Thales, serves as a reference customer and cooperatively stages these comparative tests.

Document Actual
Customer Value Provided

Demonstrating superior value is necessary, but it is no longer enough in today's business world. Suppliers also must document the cost savings and incremental profits that offerings actually have delivered to customers. Thus, suppliers work with customers to define the measures on which they will track the cost savings or incremental profit produced and then, after a suitable period of time, work with customer managers to document the actual results.

These tools, which we term *value documenters*, are used to further refine suppliers' customer value models, to create value case histories, to enable customer managers to get credit for the cost savings and incremental profit produced, and to enhance the credibility of the value demonstrations (because customer managers know that the supplier is willing to return later to document the actual value received). Value documenters are straightforward extensions of value calculators, such as the one in figure 4-2, with the addition of a "Realized value" column next to the "Demonstrated value" column (i.e., the Customer company column in the figure) to provide comparisons between the demonstrated value estimates and the actual value delivered.

Value case histories are another tool that suppliers doing business based on value, such as Nijdra Groep in the Netherlands and Applied Industrial Technologies, use. As mentioned earlier, value case histories are written accounts that document the cost savings or added value that reference customers have received from using a supplier's market offering.

Quaker Chemical Documents Actual Cost Savings

Quaker Chemical believes so much in the necessity of documenting actual cost savings that it has made that idea a part of its value proposition. Its Web site notes: "To us, 'value proposition' defines a sales offer that includes our advantaged products, the application of our process and technology knowledge, and demonstration in hard currency of the value of our recommendations. We've been compiling case after case to prove the value of our approach."

A hot mill operation was looking for improvements in the surface quality of the sheet steel it produced and the operating life of its equipment, as well as savings in electrical power and increases in productivity. Quaker proposed and implemented an entirely new roll-bite lubrication system, including the application equipment, the control equipment, the lubricant, and a weekly maintenance contract. The total cost to the customer was less than $350,000 per year. This system generated documented savings of more than $1.5 million in the first year alone, proving the value of the Quaker approach.

A major producer of automotive steel wanted to reduce costs and improve product quality in its pickling and cold rolling operations. Because Quaker understood the processes so well, it saw a way to reduce consumption of process chemicals, water, and waste treatment chemicals. Quaker proposed a solution management program providing around-the-clock coverage by an on-site team of Quaker solution technicians and a program manager. The price the customer paid for a three-year contract was $1.2 million, while the total documented operational savings for the same period were $3.8 million.

Just as Quaker does, when we say "documented," we mean that customer managers are willing to sign off on the cost savings or added revenue and profit that doing business with the supplier has produced. It is not just the supplier itself claiming it provided savings or added value, it is the customers confirming them. What a tremendous way to substantiate a value proposition!

Demonstrating and Documenting Value Benefits Grainger and Its Customers

Pharma Labs (a disguised name) is a rapidly growing pharmaceutical manufacturer. At one of its largest plants—a facility with 380 employees—purchasing managers were questioning whether to outsource their procurement of maintenance, repair, and operating (MRO) supplies and their inventory management processes. During a routine sales call, the Grainger account manager learned of the managers' concerns and arranged a half-day meeting with the vice president of operations, the purchasing manager, and the maintenance manager at that facility. He asked two Grainger Consulting Services (GCS) managers to attend this meeting, thinking that GCS might be of assistance.

Following the meeting, GCS proposed that it perform what it calls a "baseline assessment," which documents the total costs of MRO supplies management, and then, following that assessment, that it offer Pharma managers some strategic recommendations about how they could improve their operations. GCS told Pharma Labs that the assessment and the strategy development would take six to twelve weeks to complete and would cost $45,000. Pharma management agreed to the proposal.

To begin, GCS put together a case team, which consisted of a consulting manager, a consultant, and a business analyst. Pharma Labs formed a steering committee and a project team. The steering committee was composed of the relevant department heads—such as maintenance, purchasing, manufacturing, inventory management, management information systems, and finance—and was responsible for project oversight and strategy development. The project team had members from each of the departments on the steering committee and was responsible for working with the GCS case team.

Generally, GCS looks for the elements of its customer value models in four primary areas: processes (from how the need for items is identified to how invoices are paid); products (product price, usage factors, brand standardization, and application); inventory (on-hand value and carrying costs); and suppliers (performance, consolidation, and value-adding services provided). In each area GCS defines value and cost-saving elements (such as freight and courier charges and the cost of overtime); specifies the measures for the elements (such as procurement cost per purchase order, number of suppliers, and inventory accuracy); collects the data and analyzes it; and specifies measures for monitoring performance. At Pharma Labs, the measures for monitoring performance included supply expenditures, number of suppliers, and transaction volume.

In a baseline assessment, GCS uses process mapping and activity-based costing to build customer value models, drawing on proprietary databases that the company has built from its findings in past engagements. At Pharma Labs, GCS applied its activity-based costing approach to identify procurement costs across all typical functional areas—purchasing, maintenance, receiving, and accounts payable. These identified costs were generally in line with costs tracked in the GCS databases.

In any analysis GCS attempts to use the customer's electronic data whenever possible (the team usually attempts to get one year's worth of data). Early on, the case team makes a site visit to examine that data and to assess how accurate and complete it is. In the case of Pharma Labs, GCS analyzed two years of purchasing and accounts payable data, as well as six months of procurement card data. The data provided GCS and Pharma Labs with insights about the potential for consolidating the number of products Pharma Labs purchased regularly from various suppliers. It also suggested how Pharma Labs might consolidate its purchases in return for lower prices and greater value-adding services from its remaining suppliers.

At Pharma Labs, as in most GCS engagements, the case team also had to do an invoice analysis—actually inspecting past invoices to gather usable data—to validate the electronic data and to provide additional line-item product detail when available. The level of detail that the customer has is usually not adequate. Its system may contain only aggregated purchase-order information, showing only how much was paid in total. Complicating the task further, invoices themselves often have incomplete item descriptions that make it difficult to determine exactly what was purchased.

The GCS team also found from its inventory analysis that Pharma Labs had no records of the amount of inventory on hand or how it was used. Inventory levels were extremely high—the team later found that Pharma Labs had more than $1 million of slow-moving inventory—but no actual system was in place to track and manage the items.

The GCS case team supplemented its analyses by interviewing the Pharma project team members. In these interviews GCS shared its preliminary findings, tried to uncover anything that it might have overlooked, and learned what the Pharma managers themselves perceived to be potential areas of improvement. The interviews were, in fact, fruitful, alerting GCS and Pharma managers to at least one significant finding in the procurement area: Pharma lab technicians played an unusually large role in the procurement process, handling some routine purchasing, maintaining detailed handwritten logs of all transactions, receiving the items into inventory, and managing that inventory. The GCS value model showed that Pharma Labs was spending 30 percent of its procurement costs—or the equivalent of nearly three full-time positions—on lab technicians who could be redeployed from this purchasing function to more value-adding activities in their intended function. Pharma Labs eventually signed a supply agreement with another company, which, in return, put one of its people on site to manage this procurement process.

After GCS completes a baseline assessment, it then tries to specify improvements that the customer can make in six to twelve months. It also works with the customer to formulate changes in the strategy for MRO supplies management.

GCS identified at least $327,000 in total cost savings on the $6.1 million Pharma Labs was spending yearly on MRO supplies, including the costs of acquiring and managing them. These projected cost savings came about through the consolidation of suppliers and product-spending reductions ($165,000), inventory reductions ($72,000), and process improvements ($90,000). For example, GCS recommended that Pharma Labs dramatically consolidate its MRO supplies purchases. Pharma Labs agreed and initiated a national account agreement with Grainger. In return, Grainger provided Pharma Labs with an on-site representative to manage the purchase and inventory processes at the company. This allowed a Pharma maintenance technician who had been spending 100 percent of his time purchasing MRO supplies to return to performing value-adding maintenance activities.

What were the ultimate results of Grainger's work with Pharma Labs? At the end of the first year GCS and Pharma Labs started working together, they jointly conducted an audit of achieved cost savings, which were found to be $387,000 during the first six months after implementing the proposed changes. What's more, for the whole year, Grainger sales to Pharma Labs increased sevenfold—from $50,000 to $350,000. The next year, sales nearly doubled—to $650,000. Clearly, a better understating of value created substantial benefits for each company.[5]

FIVE

Tailor Market Offerings

Creating Naked Solutions with Options

MANY SUPPLIERS in business markets conclude that they're in a commodity business. We contend that this conclusion is most often misleading because it is myopic and premature. These suppliers think too narrowly about the core product or service they provide to business customers. It is true that the steel plates, letters of credit, or chemicals that they provide may be nearly, or exactly, the same as other suppliers'. Yet the market offerings that customers purchase from these suppliers are typically much more than simply the core product or service. And these suppliers have not investigated in any methodical way, such as through the customer value research we advocate, how their market offerings are different from competitors', what such differences are worth to customers, or what changes they might make in the offerings that at least some customers would find valuable.[1]

While the core products (or core services) of alternative suppliers may be essentially interchangeable, these market offerings contain many supplementary services, programs, and systems that enhance the value of the core product and provide additional value to customers. Such augmenting services, programs, and systems play an increasingly prominent role in setting suppliers apart from one another in business markets (see "Examples of Augmenting Services, Programs, and Systems"). For ease of exposition, we will refer to them as "supplementary services," or simply "services." So, before suppliers conclude that they are in a commodity business, they need to carefully examine the differences between their offerings' supplementary services and their competitors' to obtain estimates of the value that customers receive from such services.

Unfortunately, a common strategy in business markets is for suppliers to bundle supplementary services with their core products. As a result, customers tend to receive these services for free, often with virtually no limits on consumption, if they purchase the company's core product. No real analysis is done to understand (1) the value of these services for customers, (2) how they may be valuable for some customers but not for others, and (3) how they may be a source of differentiation.

In this chapter we discuss tailoring market offerings as the process of differentially putting products, services, programs, and systems together in ways that create the greatest value for targeted market segments and customer firms. It is a strategy that enables suppliers to act more like value merchants, providing managed variation in their market offerings that customers are willing to pay for. Tailoring market offerings requires offering naked solutions with options, refining targeting, and becoming more flexible in offerings.

Offer Naked Solutions with Options

Senior managers responsible for business markets must start with the realization that no matter how finely they segment a market, some residual variation in the product and service requirements of segment members will remain. That is, even though customers

Examples of Augmenting Services, Programs, and Systems

Services

Fulfillment: availability assurance, emergency delivery, installation, training, maintenance, disposal/recycling

Technical: specification, testing and analysis, troubleshooting, problem solving, calibration, customer productivity improvement

Programs

Economic: terms and conditions; deals, discounts, allowances, and rebates/bonuses; warranty; guaranteed cost savings

Relationship: advice and consulting, design, process engineering, product and process redesign, analysis of cost and performance, joint marketing research, comarketing and copromotion

Systems

Linking: order management Intranet, automated replenishment and vendor-managed inventory, enterprise resource planning, computerized maintenance management

Efficacy: information and design assistance intranet, expert systems, integrated logistics management, asset management, responsiveness systems

---

within a segment may be essentially the same in many of their requirements and preferences, they remain different in others. Suppliers can choose to ignore this residual or remaining variation with increasingly difficult consequences, or they can choose to take advantage of it by building flexibility into their market offerings.

Flexible market offerings consist of naked solutions, with options, for each market segment. A *naked solution* is the bare minimum of products and services that all customers in a market segment value. Naked solutions provide the supplier with a highly price-competitive alternative for those customers that simply want the minimum at the lowest price. The supplier puts together a set of well-chosen *options* for each naked solution, which are product enhancements and services that some, but not all, customers in the segment value. These options are offered separately for those customers that do value them and are willing to compensate the supplier for providing them.

In the past, suppliers either ignored or were unable to deal with variation between customers, choosing instead to provide standard bundles or packages of products and services designed to meet the needs of the average customer within each segment. Even worse, in many instances, suppliers have provided essentially the same vanilla offering across all segments. Thus, in business markets, a number of suppliers segment the market and then proceed to provide much the same, if not exactly the same, offerings to each segment. As the marketing manager for a large chemical company said to us, "For 90 percent of our customers, we offer the identical mix of support services."[2]

As a result, some customers feel that they are forced to pay for services they do not require, while others do not get the depth of services they require, even if they are willing to pay extra. Having a standard bundled offer for all customers also results in many customers subsidizing a few of the customers. For example, an analysis of customer profitability at one supplier demonstrated that the most profitable 20 percent of customers were responsible for 225 percent of the firm's profits; the next 70 percent of customers were responsible for 0 percent of profits; and the last 10 percent of customers were generating negative 125 percent of the firm's profits! Why was this occurring?[3]

The most profitable customers were those that had less leverage in negotiating price and used relatively little of the supplier's "free" supplementary services. Because the price paid by these customers was relatively high and the cost to serve them was relatively low, they were highly profitable for the supplier. On the other hand, those customers with whom the supplier lost money were the large-volume customers that had squeezed a low price and consumed a large proportion of the supplier's supplementary services. When this kind of customer cross-subsidization occurs, sooner or later, someone becomes aware of it and targets the highly profitable customers. If these customers are successfully poached, the first supplier is left with large money-losing customers and finally forced to confront this implicit inequity.

Naked solutions end the bad practice of forcing customers that do not value and do not use the supplementary services to subsidize those customers that do value them and consume a disproportionate amount. It also enables the supplier to offer greater amounts or higher levels of services to those customers that require them and are willing to compensate a supplier for providing. While suppliers often develop different versions of their core product or service for different customer segments, the strategy of varying supplementary services both across and within customer segments is still relatively rare.

Refine Targeting

Progressive suppliers in business markets practice finer-grained market segmentation to better understand how customer requirements and preferences, and thus the value of the market offering, vary. They find that conventional bases of segmentation, such as industry and customer size, may be a useful start but do not provide enough insight for making targeting decisions. So they further segment the market using progressive bases—such as application, customer capabilities, usage situations, and customer contribution to profitability—and then refine and pinpoint those segments and even subsegments that are of the greatest interest to target.

Flexible market offerings then allow suppliers to capitalize on any remaining variation within target segments by letting customers further tailor the offering to their own requirements and preferences. In doing so, customers select the way of doing business that is most valuable to them while being profitable to the supplier, the ultimate goal of targeting. Figure 5-1 conveys the recent flexible market offerings of KLM Cargo, a business unit of KLM Royal Dutch Airlines. By providing a base level of service and optional higher levels for its market offerings, KLM Cargo enables customers to tailor their service level to their own performance requirements. In doing so, the company has been able to obtain a larger share of customers' business.[4]

Progressive suppliers recognize that within targeted market segments, there are likely subsegments of customers that have different preferences in the way they want to do business with a supplier. Probably the most common is the distinction between customers that prefer to do business on a transactional basis versus a collaborative basis.

Differentiating Transactional from Collaborative Customers

Transactional customers purposely share their business among several suppliers in an attempt to gain further price concessions and prefer to maintain an arm's-length relationship with vendors. In contrast, *collaborative customers* are willing to reduce the number of suppliers they do business with to gain demonstrable cost savings or added value. They are also willing to consider changing how they do business with their remaining suppliers in exchange for cost savings.

A progressive supplier recognizes customers' different relationship preferences and responds with flexible market offerings. As an illustration, consider the service portion of Baxter Healthcare Corporation's market offering to two segments of interest: transactional hospital customers that do business with Baxter on

FIGURE 5-1

The flexible market offering of KLM Cargo

Our Products

KLM Cargo offers services to a wide range of customers, each with their specific needs. To respond to these needs, KLM Cargo has developed a comprehensive package of more than twenty products, grouped under seven product ranges. The destinations that KLM Cargo offers for these services differ per product and have been aligned with the global transport flows of the corresponding industries and markets.

For more information visit our website at www.klmcargo.com

Speed		The Select products offer 4-speed options for general cargo. Select Crucial for small express shipments, Select 100 offers the earliest possible arrival at destination, Select 300 offers standard acceptance & availability times at a competitive rate, Select 500 offers economy rates for non-urgent shipments.	Select	Crucial 100 300 500
Condition	**Perishable**	The Fresh products are designed for the temperature controlled transport of perishables. Fresh Regular protects perishables against temperature extremes. Fresh Cool actively maintains freshness of temperature sensitive perishables. Fresh Supercool keeps highly sensitive perishables in a constant temperature-controlled environment using special containers.	Fresh	Regular Cool Supercool
	Pharmaceutical	The Control products are dedicated to the careful and safe transport of medicals and pharmaceuticals. Control Room provides protection from extreme temperatures. Control Chill gives a transport temperature between 2-8 degrees Celcius. Control Constant uses special containers capable of maintaining every required temperature within the range of -20 to +20 degrees Celcius.	Control	Room Chill Constant
Specials — **Care**	**Valuable**	The Secure products are designed for valuable cargo. Secure Val is the full security service for gold, diamonds, banknotes, etc. Secure Vic is for theft sensitive goods such as mobile phones and high-value branded products. Secure Art provides special handling for paintings and sculptures.	Secure	Val Vic Art
	Animal	The Fit products offer transport of live animals with the highest possible care: e.g. horses, day-old chicks, tropical fish, dogs and cats. Experienced staff and dedicated equipment ensure the well-being, comfort and safety of all animals and people involved. In addition, KLM Cargo arranges special animal transport between zoo's.	Fit	Horses Chix Fish Pets Specials
Mail		Connect offers airmail services, focussing on speed and reliability. Connect Primail is based on requirements for first Class and EMS shipments. Connect Normail is the standard product, connecting with the Services Airmail Lifted (SAL) and Connect Boxmail is a container-based product for bulk airmail deliveries. Connect Diplomatic offers a dedicated service for diplomatic shipments.	Connect	Primail Normail Boxmail Diplomatic
Aerospace		Advance offers standardized and tailor-made full logistics solutions for customers in the aerospace industry. These services can range from warehousing to customs expertise, from specialized packaging to speed transportation of engines and parts, and of course 24/7 Aircraft on Ground service when every minute counts.	Advance	Aerospace

KLM
cargo

Source: KLM Cargo. Used with permission.

---

an order-by-order basis and strategic customers, which are hospitals that have committed to a closer relationship with Baxter (see table 5-1). Baxter constructed these offerings to provide ordinary and extraordinary levels of service, programs, and systems that reinforce its commitment to fulfilling strategic customers' requirements and to enhancing their medical services and financial performance. Even programs that are optional and charged for separately, such as Baxter Corporate Consulting, reflect this commitment

TABLE 5-1

Baxter Healthcare's market offerings to two segments: Transactional and strategic hospital customers

MARKET OFFERING ELEMENT	SEGMENT	
Services	Transactional customer	Strategic customer
Product returns	standard	standard
Technical assistance	standard	standard
Single point of contact	not offered	standard
Future disease incidence forecast	not offered	option
.		
.		
.		
Programs		
Price deals	standard	standard
Corporate customer bonus (financial incentive)	not offered	standard
Executive perspectives	not offered	standard
Consolidated purchasing report summary	not offered	standard
Access program	not offered	option
Baxter Corporate Consulting	not offered	option
.		
.		
.		
Systems		
ASAP order-entry system	standard	standard
Comdisco technology assessment	not offered	standard
ValueLink stockless inventory program	option	option
Comdisco asset management system	option	option
.		
.		
.		

Source: James C. Anderson and James A. Narus, *Business Market Management*, 2nd ed., © 2004, 186. Reprinted by permission of Pearson Education, Inc., Upper Saddle River, NJ.

because they provide value or savings that far exceed their cost to the strategic customer.[5]

Bringing Discipline to Supplementary Services

Businesses that have market offerings as well articulated and well managed as Baxter's are rare. More often, managers' understanding of the services, programs, and systems that their business offers within and across market segments is piecemeal, uneven, and inaccurate. For this reason, managers from all functional areas that interact with the customers in some way should take part in a structured process to determine the market offerings presently provided to each segment. These managers should meet as a group, and a facilitator should systematically take them through the various kinds of services, programs, and systems a business might offer, such as those listed in the box "Examples of Augmenting Services, Programs, and Systems." For each one, the managers should be asked, "Are you doing something like this?" As a follow-up question, the facilitator should ask, "Are you doing this sometimes for some customers?"

In most cases, a systematic examination of the supplementary services reveals that firms are inconsistent about what they offer as standard at the package price and what they market as an option, for which customers pay separately. Senior managers are surprised at the extent of unmanaged variation or ad hoc deviations (from the agreed-on strategies and tactics) their firms provide. All too often, suppliers find that their sales forces give away service options for free at the end of the year to meet sales quotas. In doing so, they cloud customer expectations of what services are standard and what are optional. Suppliers may also discover that certain customers are adept in circumventing charges, perhaps through knowing whom to call for a favor or special treatment.[6]

Understanding the Value and Costs of Supplementary Services

Before supplier managers can formulate flexible market offerings for each segment, they need to estimate the value of each service and the cost to provide it. This knowledge would seem fundamental. However, few businesses have undertaken any formal value or cost assessments. So how do leading-edge firms measure the value of their augmenting services?

Greif Inc., which manufactures fiber and plastic drums, routinely conducts what it calls "cost-in-use studies" to document the incremental cost savings, and thus the superior value, that a customer gains by using Greif products and services rather than a competitor's. To add credibility to the results, one of Greif's technical service managers works with customer managers to complete the research. In addition to examining manufacturing, team members undertake a series of process flow analyses in which they diagram the customer's business operations and estimate its current costs.

From these estimates, Greif managers brainstorm system solutions for the customer. For example, they might envision a complete materials handling system, including just-in-time deliveries and drum recycling. Then Greif gives the customer a variety of service alternatives along with estimates of cost savings. In this way, customers can make informed purchase decisions based on the worth of system solutions proposed to them.

How do progressive companies understand the service costs associated with their market offerings? To eliminate the problems associated with fuzzy services and the tendency of sales reps to bury costs, a manufacturer of food additives and seasonings revamped its service delivery and planning systems. For starters, the company more precisely defined its services and the levels at which it offered each one. Its sales force, which was composed of highly trained technical representatives, was required to handle all minor services, such as basic problem solving. Charges for such services account for a portion of the total yearly budget allotted to each sales representative.

All major services, such as detailed technical problem solving, were offered on a project basis and delivered by technical experts from departments such as customer service. Either the customer directly paid for the project, which was preferred, or a charge was placed against the allotted discretionary budget of its sales representative. At the beginning of every year, managers at the manufacturer constructed a plan for each major customer account that defined financial and volume targets and specified the levels of services the manufacturer would provide. At the end of the year, the managers reviewed these plans, examined service costs and account profitability, and recommended changes in the level of account services for the next year.

Suppliers have difficulty in activity-based costing of shared resources, which tend to characterize the provision of services, programs, and systems. Yet significant progress is being made in activity-based costing for these kinds of applications. Robert Kaplan and Steven Anderson have introduced *time equations,* which enable activity-based costing models to reflect how order and activity characteristics cause variation in processing times. A time equation expresses in simple words and mathematical operators the minutes to perform an activity and how those minutes are affected by variations in the activity, such as providing differing levels of service. Consider an example that Kaplan and Anderson provide to capture the variation in minutes required to package a chemical for shipment to a customer, depending on the requirement for special packaging or mode of transportation:

Packaging

time = 0.5 + 6.5 [if special packaging is required] + 2.0
[if shipping is by air]

This time estimate in minutes is then multiplied by the cost per minute of supplying that capacity to provide a cost estimate for order packaging. This time equation tool for simplifying activity-based costing is strikingly compatible with the value word equation tool presented in chapter 3. Together, they provide suppliers with methodical, yet practical means of precisely expressing and estimating the value and the cost of providing supplementary services.[7]

Become More Flexible in Offerings

When formulating flexible market offerings for different segments, suppliers can choose from three strategic alternatives for deploying each service element: do not market the service, market it as standard (with no charge), or market it as an option (with a charge). Each service itself has one of three statuses: the service is a new one (meaning that it has not been previously marketed by the supplier, although it may have been offered by a competitor), it is an existing standard service, or it is an existing optional service.

We cross service status with service element deployment to provide nine unique combinations. A useful way to organize these nine resulting strategies is a flexible market offering strategy matrix, which we show in figure 5-2. This matrix can provide a systematic picture of the nature and balance of a supplier's market offering. It also can promote further inquiry and strategy development, as when, for example, managers find that one or more cells are empty.

Reevaluate Existing Standard Services

Because the overriding philosophy is to keep the standard offering as naked as possible, only those service, program, and system

FIGURE 5-2

Flexible market offering strategy matrix for services, programs, and systems

Service element status	Service element deployment		
	Do not market	Market as standard	Market as option
Existing standard service	Prune from standard offering	Retain in standard offering	Recast as surcharge option
Existing optional service	Discontinue option	Enhance standard offering	Retain as value-added option
New service	Keep on shelf	Augment standard offering	Introduce as value-added option

Source: James C. Anderson and James A. Narus, *Business Market Management*, 2nd ed., © 2004, 191. Reprinted by permission of Pearson Education, Inc., Upper Saddle River, NJ.

elements that all firms within a segment highly value should be standard. The first place to put this philosophy into practice is by reevaluating the existing standard services. By discontinuing, or pruning, some of these and recasting others as options, supplier managers retain the subset of services that will serve as the base of an updated standard offering. *Prune* here is used in the horticultural sense, trimming a tree or shrub to improve its vitality, rather than in the dried-plum sense, which is used to improve vitality in quite a different way!

Prune from the standard offering. Suppliers are often far more reluctant to discontinue existing services than they are to add services. Nonetheless, managers need to scrutinize existing elements for pruning candidates. One source is those services that most segment members rarely use. The customers that still value the service are so few that it is not worthwhile for the supplier to continue to offer it. In the interest of these customers, though, the supplier can sometimes outsource the service or suggest another firm that provides it.

Following detailed investigations, a chemical manufacturer learned, to its chagrin, that while each of its 186 services continued to incur annual fixed costs, many had not been used in the past year. Its managers responded by pruning a large number of them. Many customers didn't even realize the services were discontinued.

Retain in the standard offering. A supplier sometimes retains services in the standard offering even if they are not ones that are highly valued by all firms in a segment. The success of certain services, in terms of their value or cost, depends on their widespread usage by customers. Web-based order placement, Web-based tracking systems, and logistics management systems are examples.

Service elements that a supplier cannot readily differentiate from those of competitors are candidates for including in the standard offering. Such elements are often regarded as standard in industry market offerings and make up a substantial part of the naked offering. The challenge in offering these parity services is to have customers perceive their value as not being significantly less than competitors' comparable services but at the same time to manage their costs below those of the competition. Why? Because customers typically do not place much value on these services, they do not factor into customers' decisions about changing suppliers as long as they are minimally acceptable.

Recast as a surcharge option. Supplier managers report that recasting a standard service as a surcharge option is the most difficult of the nine strategies to implement. Customers may react angrily when told they must now pay for something they had expected to get for free. It is even more difficult when competitors continue to market the service for free as part of a standard offering. Nowhere is this more of a problem than in industries characterized by high levels of fixed costs, such as commodity industrial chemicals and fully integrated steel mills. In such industries managers hesitate to implement any scheme that may result in reduced sales volume because it may jeopardize their ability to reach profitable capacity-utilization levels. As a result, they routinely add services to retain volume and rarely drop any.

Infrequently performed services that deliver value at specific points in time—such as training, installation, and retrofitting—are perhaps the best candidates for redeploying as surcharge options. By marketing these services as value-added options, suppliers retain the business of customers that still derive value from them and are willing to pay for them. Often this provides a real test for services that customers claim have no value for them (or are said to be the same as those obtainable for free from other suppliers) but that suppliers believe are worth something to them. Depending on the market response, suppliers can either continue these services as value-added options or discontinue them.

Leading supplier firms use a variety of approaches to recast services as value-added options. To make the overhaul of its standard service package more palatable to its customers, one specialty chemical company implemented a variation of this strategy. Along with specialty organic chemicals, the company offers a variety of services including laboratory support, field consulting, on-site testing, and educational seminars—all of which are costly. Realizing that its customers value and use these services differently, the company offers customers a variety of levels for each service. If a customer purchases a minimum amount of products each year, it receives basic levels of services along with the standard offering. If that same customer wants to receive a higher level of service, it can either increase its annual purchases to a prespecified amount or pay extra. Thus, some level of each service is available with every standard offering. Customers that place greater value on the service have the option to buy more.

As a prelude to making some previously standard services value-added options, a large computer company began listing a charge for the provided services, which was then subtracted with the notation "Do not pay this." An accompanying letter explained that the company was pleased to have been able to provide the field service and stated what it estimated this service was worth to the customer, using market-based rates for independent industry consultants. Why would a supplier employ this tactic, which we call a *pseudo-invoice*? Such an approach enabled the company to establish the value of its services in the minds of customers and opened the possibility for charging for those services in the future. Thus, a sharp distinction can be drawn between offering an element separately, even as an invoice reduction "no charge," and simply burying it within the standard package.

Another alternative is to have the customer pay, in full or in part, for whatever options it values with "bonus dollars" earned from doing business with the supplier. Strategic customers accrued "Baxter dollars" based on the amount of and growth in their purchases from Baxter Healthcare, which they then applied to any of a number of optional services, programs, and systems. In this way, strategic hospital customers used a common resource,

Baxter dollars, to tailor the company's market offering to their own individual requirements.

Reexamine Optional Services

Next, supplier managers should reexamine existing optional services to determine whether they should be discontinued, used to enhance the standard offering, or continued as options. As was the case with reevaluating the standard package, evaluating and constructing options menus should begin with a deliberate attempt to prune existing optional services. Optional services that were once good sources of revenue for the supplier but are no longer used enough to justify their fully allocated costs are pruning candidates. Similarly, services whose cost has outstripped customers' willingness to pay for them (due to changes in technology, the expertise required, or insurance risk) are also candidates. For example, because of insurance risk, most manufacturers are unwilling to provide transportation for drums of solvents, even for an additional delivery fee. As was the case with pruning standard services, suppliers sometimes can help customers that still need these services by outsourcing them from other firms.

At times, suppliers may fold into standard offerings services that they have marketed as options. And if the core product of the market offering is regarded as a commodity, suppliers can enhance the standard offering as a means of differentiating themselves from competitors. But be warned: many suppliers think that customers do business on the basis of which supplier has the best or most extensive set of services, which is not necessarily true because customers within a segment will vary in how they value these services. Such suppliers are often driven to offer more elements in their standard offering than necessary.

Instead, suppliers should consider trimming the standard offering to the naked solution, offering a set of options and letting customers pay, in full or in part, for whatever options they value with bonus dollars. The more customers consolidate their purchases with the supplier, the more bonus dollars they earn and the more services they can purchase. Not only does this allow customers to tailor the supplier's market offering to their own particular requirements, but it reinforces that they do not have to pay for services they do not want. To underscore the value of the services it offers, a supplier can promise to give customers cash for any unused bonus dollars at the end of the agreement, as Baxter Healthcare did.

Build Flexibility with New Services

What are the sources of new services? Some suppliers rely on their own strengths and capabilities to identify new services to offer. Another source is focusing on the cost structures and strategic imperatives of targeted customers. What new services can the supplier innovate that will assist these customers in their own initiatives to lower costs or improve performance?

Because they have not been offered in the past, new services do not carry the baggage of customer expectations about how a supplier should provide them (i.e., whether or not those services should carry a fee). Thus, new services provide the best means to build flexibility into market offerings. While suppliers should try to preserve new services as stand-alone options, at times those companies may elect not to offer them or use them to enhance the standard offering.

Keep it on the shelf. Suppliers may decide not to offer a new element because of a variety of issues. It may be that customers have not yet recognized an element's value, the cost of providing it is still too high, or the present element it would replace is still deemed adequate. Akzo Nobel Industrial Coatings (ANIC) provides an example. It anticipated greater environmental concerns about current painting technologies and invested substantial time and resources in the technological development of a process for water-borne paint application.

ANIC consulted with its customers on changing to this more environmentally benign technology. Unfortunately, although many customers were interested to learn that ANIC possessed this capability, no one was willing to pay extra for it. ANIC managers believed that customers would not value the process until environmental protection laws required a significant reduction in solvent emissions. As a result, they decided to keep the technology on the shelf until customer value increased.

Augment the standard offering. Suppliers sometimes enhance standard offerings with new services. When suppliers segment the market by relationships, managers look for new elements that will sustain and invigorate collaborative relationships. One way is to add new services that anticipate and are responsive to customers' changing requirements. Okuma, a Japanese builder of computer numerical control machine tools, provides an example. In one year, it introduced a twenty-four-hour parts shipment guarantee, and in the next, it began to sell a guaranteed trade-in program. Okuma management believed that in addition to being responsive to a changing marketplace, the practice forced its distributors and employees to be more efficient—now they had to learn how to ship parts anywhere in the United States in twenty-four hours. It also gave the sales force something new and interesting to discuss during sales presentations.

Shrewd suppliers also add new services to standard offerings to stymie competitors. The industrial division of Baxter Scientific Products (BSP), for example, deliberately seeks out new services that customers value and that BSP can perform better or offer more inexpensively than the competition.[8] By bundling such new services in with the standard offering, BSP forces competitors to choose from a series of unpleasant alternatives. If competitors decline to offer the service altogether, BSP can tout its unique service to customers as an extra benefit of doing business with the company. If competitors attempt to match BSP and offer the service, they will incur both added costs and time delays associated with learning how to deliver the new service.

New elements that also are likely candidates for inclusion in the standard offering are those for which (1) most of the costs are incurred in their initial development or deployment; (2) continuing costs vary relatively little over the number of customers actually using the element; or (3) usage of the element in some way reduces the supplier's own costs.

Introduce as a value-added option. Offering new elements separately provides value-added options for customers that seek them and allows suppliers to readily gauge interest in new services, programs, and systems. For example, although R.R. Donnelley's traditional business has focused on printing, binding, film preparation, and prepress work, its management believes that future growth and profits will come from innovative services, such as database management, consulting and training, dimensional and talking ads, direct marketing, layout systems, and mapping services. To test their viability in the marketplace, Donnelley has offered these services as value-added options.

Break Away from the Pack

In our management practice research, a number of managers wistfully expressed a desire for change but were concerned about what competitors would do. These managers believed their competitors were looking to improve profitability too but that they wouldn't match a move to make more flexible market offerings. In addition, these managers had timing and discipline concerns. Before taking up these last two concerns, though, we consider breaking away as a means of countering competitors' dubious parity claims.

One way to break away from the pack (which also works for services included in the standard offering) is to guarantee outcomes based on the service. The larger and more complicated the list of services a firm markets, the more likely it is that competitors will claim, "We can do that." When this occurs, savvy marketers respond by transforming service claims into guarantees. For instance, when

Okuma's competitors began to promise rapid delivery, Okuma announced its twenty-four-hour shipment guarantee. If a customer orders a part and it is not shipped in twenty-four hours, the customer gets the part for free. Greif Inc. takes the guarantee one step further, introducing a guaranteed cost-savings program. If a customer requests that it be given a 5 percent price cut, the division guarantees to find at least a 5 percent cost savings. This is formalized into a written contract. If the customer doesn't realize the 5 percent savings, Greif agrees to pay the difference. If more than 5 percent of savings is found, the customer gets to keep it all. To date, Greif has had no problem delivering as guaranteed. Furthermore, managers find that it's a great way to turn discussions away from price.

Knowing when to break away and become more flexible in market offerings is difficult. Is there an advantage to being the first, or is it better to be a rapid follower? To be an industry paradigm breaker, the first supplier must have tough resolve and be willing to take the heat. An intermediate strategy is to pilot-test flexible market offerings in one of two ways: either (1) add two new services but offer them as options or (2) pick two services from the present industry standard package and unbundle them, making them surcharge options. Going against industry practice is the first step toward an industry paradigm shift.

Many companies refrain from implementing flexible market offerings because they fear they will lose certain customers by requiring them to pay extra for optional services. Instead, managers might adopt the philosophy of firms that have implemented flexible market offerings and found that, while they lost some accounts, they have gained new business because their market offerings now more closely meet customer requirements at reasonable prices. Other suppliers that have implemented flexible market offerings have found that they now get a better return on their resources by focusing them on the segments and customers that value those resources.

Timing is always a concern. ANIC initiated its customer contribution to profitability approach in Europe about ten years ago.

Because revamping service offerings and pricing them to get an equitable return on the value provided was not only new to the industry but internally controversial, ANIC decided to implement it first in the Netherlands and Germany, "home" markets where ANIC was strongest. It then rolled out the approach to northern Europe. Southern Europe, the last to be converted, proved to be the most difficult market to bring around because its sales forces anticipated decreases in their commission incomes and resisted the change. Although ANIC lost some customers after reducing its offering of free services, overall, its perseverance resulted in stable sales volume at significantly better profitability.

A final, paramount consideration to succeed in what we have recommended is this: suppliers must have the discipline to operate within the imposed structures of flexible market offerings. Maintaining this discipline requires developing a difficult-to-acquire customer skill: adroitly saying no to some customers. Flexible market offerings provide customers with managed options from which they can choose, but suppliers must be willing to say no to those that want full-service offerings at no-frills prices.

Without this skill, flexible market offerings devolve to business as usual—that is, giving services away. Practiced deftly, it builds a reputation for the supplier within the industry as being firm, consistent, and fair. Isn't it time to break away from the pack?

Tailoring Market Offerings: Dow Corning and Xiameter

As a noteworthy case in tailoring market offerings, consider Dow Corning.[9] In 2000, it was serving its customers with seven thousand different products that were bundled with all kinds of supplementary services. Despite a leading 40 percent worldwide market share in silicones, Dow Corning was facing a number of low-cost competitors that were undercutting its prices. Rather than try to match competitors' prices and lose the price premium across its entire volume, Dow Corning decided to fight back. And it all began with research to assess what customers truly value.

A careful study of customers uncovered the following four customer segments:

1. *Customers seeking to innovate*—customers inventing state-of-the-art products, creating advanced technologies, or developing new markets. Innovation-focused customers were committed to being first to market with new applications and revolutionary products. They sought advances, even breakthroughs, in the creation of technical or market positions that did not exist.

2. *Customers seeking a productivity increase*—customers seeking off-the-shelf products with proven performance. They needed help with improving the acquisition, use, and disposal of products. From order tracking and materials handling to processing assistance and troubleshooting, they wanted dependable supply, minimal downtime, and turnkey solutions around the world.

3. *Customers seeking to reduce total cost*—customers seeking supply chain optimization for cost reduction or customer service improvement. Other areas of support included vendor-managed inventory, custom packaging, cost-in-use studies, and supply chain analysis.

4. *Customers seeking to better prices*—customers in mature industries that wanted materials and services at the best price they could get. They bought mature products in large quantities and did not require service but instead sought quality, reliability, and low prices to make them more cost effective.

The customer research led to the insight that the last segment did not value the supplementary services that Dow Corning offered. However, since the supplementary services were bundled with the product and those costs had to be recovered, the naked solution was too expensive for the last segment. Understandably, this segment refused to pay for the services it did not value and pressured for lower prices. But lowering prices for this segment without changing the fundamental market offer was problematic because then the customers from the other three segments, which truly valued the supplementary services, would also demand the same lower prices. The need for tailored market offerings was obvious.

In 2002, to serve this low-price-seeking segment, Dow Corning launched a wholly owned subsidiary called Xiameter. Xiameter realized it needed to cut its prices by 15–20 percent, which was very significant in the business markets it was serving. This could only be done profitably, though, if the costs to serve the customer were also reduced by a proportionate amount. Furthermore, it had to be launched in such a manner that it did not simply cannibalize existing sales in the other three segments. The result? Xiameter was targeted to "price-driven convenience buyers of mature silicone-based products that spend over $50,000/p.a. [per year] on silicone materials." To be both cost efficient and attractive only to price buyers, the market offering and value proposition were defined in the following manner:

- Instead of Dow Corning's fast-delivery promise, Xiameter promises a shipping date seven to twenty days from the date of order. This allows Xiameter to slot orders when there is spare capacity at Dow Corning.

- Xiameter offers no technical service. This means Xiameter does not have to invest in an expensive service capability.

- Xiameter provides no order-size flexibility for the customer. Depending on the product, customers must order full-truck, tank, or pallet loads. This enables Xiameter to run efficient logistics.

- Customers can enter their own orders on Xiameter's Web site, but if they wish to send the order by e-mail or phone, there is a $250 charge per order. This reduces customer interface costs.

- The shipping date, once set, may not be changed unless the customer is willing to pay a 5 percent surcharge. A rush order incurs a 10 percent penalty, while the order cancellation fee is 5 percent. All of this makes production planning more predictable.

- The credit terms are very tight—thirty days net, 18 percent. This reduces the working capital required.

- The product variety available is limited to 350 mature products in contrast to the 7,000 products available through Dow Corning. This limits cannibalization and focuses on those products where Dow Corning faces price competition from low-cost players.

- Product returns are accepted only if the goods are damaged.

- The worldwide pricing is available in only six major currencies so that the currency risk and exchange is limited.

To emphasize what is the same, Xiameter provides certificates of chemical equivalency for customers to demonstrate that its newly branded products are equivalent to the Dow Corning products. Thus, the core product is an exact commodity. It is the supplementary services that vary.

The results for Xiameter have been excellent. The cannibalization in the first year after launch was half of what the company had projected. While its prices are 15–20 percent lower, by having a Web-only model, it has eliminated several cost factors—like technical service, a sales force, and inventory costs—and optimized other costs, like logistics and production. In addition, the working capital requirements are low because the accounts receivable are low and inventory is minimal. Taken together, these cost savings yield an attractive return on assets. Furthermore, by using the spare capacity of the Dow Corning production lines, Xiameter also makes Dow Corning operations more efficient.

Since its launch, Xiameter has significantly contributed to Dow Corning's increase in sales—from $2.4 billion in 2001 to $3.9 billion in 2005. During the same period, Dow Corning went from a loss of $28 million to a profit of $500 million—quite a turnaround. In addition to this vastly improved financial performance, the dual-brand strategy of Dow Corning and Xiameter has helped customers more clearly see the value that Dow Corning brings with its market offering. Customers observe the contrasting value propositions and offerings for each brand, resulting in their making more-informed decisions on how they want to purchase. Thus, tailoring Dow Corning's market offerings to be responsive to customers with varying requirements and preferences certainly has paid off for the company and its customers.

Transform the Sales Force into Value Merchants

Selling on Value, Not Price

GIVING VALUE AWAY takes no particular skill. However, it is the responsibility of marketing and, especially, sales to get a fair return on the value delivered to customers. For most firms in business markets, the sales force is a substantial cost. And suppliers can't justify paying for a sales force that only sells on price. Unfortunately, too often salespeople do exactly that—they become the customer's advocate for price cuts rather than the supplier's advocate for the value provided.

In this chapter we begin by contrasting value merchants with value spendthrifts. We contend that while compensating salespeople on profitability is necessary, it is not sufficient to transform the sales force into value merchants. We then consider what suppliers must do to foster value merchants. We end with a case study on how Milliken transformed its sales force into value merchants.

Value Merchants Versus
Value Spendthrifts

A *value merchant* recognizes the supplier's own costs and the market offering's value to the customer and works to obtain a fair return for both the supplier firm and the customer firm. The value merchant stands in stark contrast to the all-too-common *value spendthrift*, who squanders the superior value of the supplier's market offerings, getting little in return. In "Are Your Salespeople Value Merchants or Value Spendthrifts?" we provide a series of paired statements that contrast value spendthrifts and value mer-

---

Are Your Salespeople Value Merchants or Value Spendthrifts?

From each of the following pairs of descriptive statements, decide which one best describes your sales force. Then put together the profile of your sales force from the statements selected.

Our salespeople:

1. Routinely trade more business for lower prices—or routinely gain more business at the same price.

2. Make unsupported claims about superior value to customers—or demonstrate and document claims about superior value in monetary terms to customers.

3. Focus on the revenue/volume component of their compensation plan—or on the gross margin/profitability component of their compensation plan.

4. Give price concessions without changes in the market offering—or give price concessions only in exchange for cost-saving reductions in the market offering.

---

chants. By candidly picking the statement in each pair that best describes your salespeople, you can construct a profile of them that indicates the extent to which they are value merchants or value spendthrifts.

Certainly, compensation significantly contributes to whether salespeople act as value merchants or value spendthrifts. Yet many suppliers have difficulty resolving what they want when constructing their sales compensation plans. A classic management practice article is entitled "On the Folly of Rewarding A, While Hoping for B."[1] In our context this refers to the folly of rewarding revenue or volume while hoping for profitability. To transform the sales force into value merchants, suppliers must have compensation plans

---

5. Complain that our prices are too high—or complain that our proof of superior value is lacking.

6. Give services away for free to close a deal—or strategically employ services to generate additional business.

7. Prefer to give quick price concessions to close deals and go on to other business—or are willing to hang tough in the negotiations to gain better profitability out of each deal.

8. Believe management pursues a capacity-driven strategy—or believe management pursues a value-driven strategy.

9. Sell primarily on price comparisons with competitors—or sell primarily on customer cost-of-ownership comparisons with competitors.

10. Tell us customers are only interested in price—or tell us customer insights to improve the value of our offerings.

---

that seamlessly reward value-selling behaviors and profitable outcomes. For value calculators and value documenters to become
the preferred way to sell, salespeople have to see how using these
tools will make successful selling easier or will make them more
money. Compensating the sales force based on profitability of accounts brings together doing business based on demonstrated and
documented superior value *and* getting a fair return on the value
delivered.

Many firms have a profitability component to their sales compensation plan. Unfortunately, often the weighting of this component relative to the revenue or volume component is insufficient
to sway salesperson preference away from pursuing revenue or
volume. This relative weighting may reflect management's own
mixed feelings about what the business should pursue, particularly in businesses with costly capacity that management wants to
fully utilize. Yet, when management is able to resolve its conflicting
feelings to make profitability count significantly more than volume or revenue, the effect on salespeople's behavior can be profound. As one manager at a chemical company remarked to us when
his firm made a change to having gross margin weighted 60 percent in its incentive compensation: "It was like giving an instant
blood transfusion to our sales force!" Before, when an offering's
price was 6¢ per pound higher than the next-best alternative, the
salesperson typically submitted a competitive price request seeking a price concession. Now, the manager related, salespeople would
instead put together a presentation to the customer justifying why
their offering was worth the 6¢ price differential.

Yet, undeniably, some businesses pursue a strategy that depends on substantial volume. The challenge is to make that volume
profitable. Consider the noteworthy example of Composites One,
a leading reseller of composite materials and equipment for customers that manufacture fiberglass and reinforced plastics for
marine, defense, and transportation uses. Composites One's sales
compensation plan consists of a good base salary plus substantial
incentive compensation, which can range from 50 percent to over

100 percent of the salesperson's base salary. The incentive compensation is based on the total gross margin dollars that each salesperson earns in his or her territory. Expenses that the salesperson can directly control and an allocation for any bad debt occurring from the salesperson's customers then are subtracted from the total gross margin dollars to yield the adjusted total gross margin dollars. The percentage of these adjusted total gross margin dollars that become the salesperson's incentive compensation vary from 8 percent to 10 percent, depending on the size of territory and number of customer accounts. With this sales compensation plan, Composites One management makes it clear to salespeople that while volume is important, total gross margin dollars are paramount.

To ensure that salespeople practice value-selling skills, suppliers may have a behavioral component as well as a profitable outcome component in their sales compensation plans. After all, even well-learned skills, if not practiced regularly, begin to decline. As time goes on without practice, this leads to a downward spiral in the salesperson's perception of his or her capability and a growing reluctance to use value-based sales tools. Thus, it is critical that salespeople demonstrate that they regularly use their value-based sales tools with customers and that they continue to build their proficiency and comfort with such tools.

At SKF, 50 percent of salespeople's incentive compensation is based on individual targets, such as the Documented Solutions Program (DSP) activities completed, sales growth in their territories, and the introduction of specific products. (DSP is a tool to demonstrate and document value created for customers.) The remaining 50 percent is based on total value added, which is defined as net profitability after subtracting the cost of capital, and is calculated based on the geographic area, business unit, and division performance. SKF, interestingly, uses the number of activities a salesperson quantifies in monetary terms using the DSP tool as its measure for compensation. It believes that the number is more important than the actual monetary amounts because it wants its salespeople to make the DSP tool a part of their daily activity.

Rockwell Automation sales engineers have a compensation plan consisting of a base salary plus an incentive. As part of the performance review, each sales engineer is required to perform a specified number of total-cost-of-ownership (TCO) assessments using the TCO Toolbox, an interactive laptop software program for demonstrating and documenting value. The TCO cases that result from these analyses are used to demonstrate increased depth of knowledge about the customers and the TCO analysis, both of which are also requirements to earn the incentive compensation.

Salespeople Who Are Able to Sell Value and Want To

How have we equipped our salespeople to be able to sell value? Why should our salespeople want to sell value? To prosper in business markets, the general manager and senior sales executive for each business should pose and be able to persuasively answer each of those questions. Yet we repeatedly find that those questions go unanswered, which undermines profitable sales growth. Without convincing answers, should senior management really expect value merchants?

Some managers mistakenly believe that the right sales compensation plan—perhaps revved up periodically with a promotion or contest—is all that is needed. We contend that suppliers must also manage two other contributors to get their salespeople to want to sell value: they must provide meaningful initial and ongoing field experience in selling value, and they also must begin and sustain a culture that celebrates value merchants.

Yet wanting to sell value without the ability to sell it will also not succeed. Some managers mistakenly believe that a value-selling sales training course, with salespeople taking turns role playing the customer, will impart whatever knowledge and skill their salespeople will need to sell value. We contend that being able to sell value depends on a pilot-tested process and value-based sales tools that salespeople are committed to using. Initial and ongoing field experience in selling value not only underpins wanting to sell value; it also underpins being able to sell value.

Fostering Value Merchants

Although many businesses have launched value-selling initiatives, most find that the results have fallen short of their expectations. Getting salespeople to change is not easy; they tend to be skeptical of new initiatives. In our management practice research, we have found very few businesses that excel at each necessary facet of fostering value merchants. In this section we draw on the collective experience of businesses that are grappling with and have achieved some success in transforming their salespeople into value merchants. We suggest a framework for transforming the sales force into value merchants, supported by examples from these businesses.

Put a Value-Selling Process and Value-Based Sales Tools in Place

Convincing salespeople to stop doing business based on price and to start doing business based on demonstrated and documented superior value depends on involving them actively and early in the process. Using a couple of the more progressive salespeople as members of the teams that are carrying out customer value research projects is essential. These salespeople contribute to conceptualizing the points of parity and points of difference, constructing the value word equations, and then gathering the data at customer sites. Because of these seasoned salespeople's contributions each step of the way, the resulting value calculators and value documenters are not viewed as a top-management-driven "black box" when the salespeople receive them. Rather, some of their peers are champions who have helped create the tools, who believe in the customer value management approach, and who take the lead in explaining to the rest of the salespeople why they ought to use the tools. The same goes for establishing and pilot testing the value-selling process.

Sales councils, which are internal advisory groups of salespeople who are respected by their peers, can play a significant role in gaining sales force commitment and support. Rockwell Automation actively involves its sales councils in the design and provisioning of its sales tools and systems. In addition to its TCO Toolbox, the company also has a reporting system that requires salespeople to provide information on the number of calls they have made, customer managers they have approached, sales presentations they have led, TCO analyses they have conducted, and orders they have obtained. Because of the sales councils' early involvement and input, they were willing to take the lead in explaining the benefits of the reporting system to the rest of the sales force and showed why complying would be worthwhile. The sales councils also provided recommendations to their peers on how and when to use the TCO Toolbox. The sales councils' early participation gave, in essence, Rockwell's sales engineers a stake in the success of the system and tool.[2]

Value-selling process. A more insightful and skillful salesperson intuitively follows a methodical process to investigate customer requirements and preferences, puts together and proposes responsive market offerings, demonstrates that they are superior to those of the competition, negotiates a fair price in return, and then makes sure that the business delivers on what the salesperson has promised the customer. The purpose of putting a value-selling process in place is to make this tacit knowledge explicit and complete so that even less insightful and less skillful salespeople can follow it consistently to produce superior results. As an example of a value-selling process, let's consider that of Kennametal.

Kennametal is a leading global supplier of tooling, engineered components, and advanced materials that are consumed in its customers' production processes. The importance of selling value stems, in part, from what Kennametal sells. At the typical customer, the cost of tooling represents only 2–4 percent of the total production costs. Thus, the value of Kennametal products and services for a given customer is not in cutting its "spend" on tooling but rather in using the tooling to drive productivity and thereby attack the other 96–98 percent of the company's production costs. In fact, Kennametal sales representatives could not get time with the customer plant management if Kennametal's value proposition was to cut cost on the 2–4 percent of tooling spend. It just wouldn't be important enough to justify the plant leadership's time. However, when the value proposition involves leveraging the tooling spend to cut double-digit percentages out of the total manufacturing cost, sales representatives are better able to gain the attention of higher management levels at the customer's operation.

Kennametal finds that having a global value-selling process in place provides a consistent, reliable, and repeatable process for continuously improving the way it does business with its customers. This process also provides a means for sharing enterprise-wide best practices for achieving greater customer loyalty and increased sales. The process consists of six steps:

1. Target customers

2. Discover needs

3. Develop a customer-specific value proposition

4. Build a detailed sales plan

5. Execute relentlessly

6. Listen and modify

The six steps are arrayed in a circle to convey that the Kennametal process is a continuing relationship. At the center of this circle is "Aggressive mindset: Refuse to lose and 100 percent share" to emphasize that Kennametal seeks 100 percent share of its targeted customers' purchase requirements and that, implemented properly, the company will not lose to its competitors.

Value-based sales tools. As we have discussed in chapter 4, management must equip its salespeople with tools that enable them to persuasively demonstrate and document the superior value of its market offerings to target customers and, in doing so, enable them to influence customer manager perceptions of what makes a fair return. We have emphasized value calculators and value case histories as sales tools. Yet, whatever form these tools take, they must provide evidence to customers about the superior value of the supplier's offering that those customers find persuasive. This evidence should be based on facts or data and should accurately reflect the customer's business. Wherever and whenever possible, this evidence should be expressed in monetary terms.

A great way to persuade prospective customers to try a supplier's offering is to share with them the experiences that other customers have had with that offering. Whether the reference customer in a value case history is named or disguised, prospective customers find the comments attributed to it credible, much more so than if the supplier itself made those statements. And knowledge of customer value is a reusable resource. So value merchants who generate knowledge of customer value by documenting it for their customers recognize that they and their peers can recast it for use as value case histories.

Getronics, an Amsterdam-based provider of information and communications technology solutions and services (with annual sales of over €4.1 billion), makes use of its value case histories by furnishing its sales representatives with a DVD set entitled *Plain Talk. Practical Solutions.* The two-pack set contains a series of professionally produced videos with descriptions of the company and its solutions, two presentations, and numerous case studies from major clients. When visiting a prospect, the sales rep can either mute the audio and give the presentation him- or herself or leave the DVD set with the client to view at a more convenient time.

While value case histories are extremely effective, it is challenging, as with any database, to keep them fresh, updated, and vital. As a result, a one-time effort to set them up is not enough. Rather, sales forces have to be motivated to use, update, and refine the value case histories database. This is what best-practice companies, such as GE Infrastructure Water & Process Technologies (W&PT), excel at doing. A pioneer in substantiating value propositions over the past decade, W&PT documents the actual results its solutions have provided to customers through its value generation planning (VGP) process and tools, which enable its field personnel to work with customers to understand their businesses and then plan, execute, and document projects that have the highest value impact for them. An online tracking tool allows W&PT and customer managers to easily monitor the execution and documented results of each project W&PT undertakes. Since it began using VGP in 1992, W&PT has documented more than a thousand case histories, accounting for $1.3 billion in customer cost savings, 24 billion gallons of water conserved, 5.5 million tons of waste eliminated, and 4.8 million tons of air emissions removed.

In addition to snapshot value-based sales tools, experienced value merchants employ a complementary value-accumulation tool that documents the value provided to a customer over time. Such a tool arms salespeople with a proactive response when customers ask, "What have you done lately?" This question often arises in account reviews. Astute suppliers create this tool, train salespersons in its use, and compensate them for taking the time to keep score on the value created in the relationship, which would otherwise be forgotten.

Even the most fantastic value-based sales tools, though, will receive little use if salespeople do not feel competent or comfortable with them. Such tools also will receive little use if salespeople do not believe that these tools will help them earn more money or make their selling efforts easier. That is why astute management makes certain that salespeople's initial experience using the tools with customers generates success and that they continue to use the tools.

Ensure Initial and Ongoing Value-Selling Experiences with Customers

Most salespeople's first exposure to using value-based sales tools to become value merchants occurs at a sales meeting, where they learn about the process and tools that their business has designed. Hopefully, this message comes from respected peers of theirs who have actively participated in the development and pilot testing of the process and tools. The next step will be sales training, when salespeople learn more about the process and attempt to use the tools. Their skill and comfort levels, though, come from using the tools in the field. This skill and comfort grow as they have to use these tools regularly and, when needed, can call on support from customer value specialists.

For such training to be meaningful, it must begin by providing a compelling reason to sell on value. SKF has found that providing its salespeople, who are accustomed to technical selling, with success stories of value selling as well as examples of failure with technical selling gets the attention of training participants. For example, the manager leading the training will share a case in which the SKF salesperson did a great job of technical selling yet lost the business on price. He then asks the training participants why this happened and how SKF could prevent such outcomes. Success stories share actual SKF cases that reinforce three outcomes of using the DSP tool: (1) salespeople are able to sell more products; (2) it dramatically increases the close rate, up to 50–60 percent; and (3) it get the salesperson away from a price discussion, with customer managers often using the DSP reports internally to justify their capital requests.

Salespeople typically gain their initial experience with value-based sales tools through role-playing exercises during the training. One salesperson plays the customer while the other is the salesperson, and then they reverse roles. For this to be meaningful, though, the roles have to be realistic and representative of actual customer experiences. SKF makes certain that the customer roles are written from real customer cases. After the role playing, participants are debriefed on how they did, talking through what went well and what did not.

Provide initial success in selling value to customers. Even though considerable effort may be put into making the role-playing exercise realistic, it is not the same as using the value-based sales tools with customers in the field. Because of this difference, suppliers that are serious about transforming their sales forces into value merchants follow up the sales training with in-the-field practice, where the salesperson receives hands-on coaching and support. This coaching and support may be provided by customer value specialists or by experienced sales managers.

SKF has its "area value champions" work one-on-one with its salespeople, spending a week driving around with them, conducting joint sales calls. Over the course of the week, the two use the DSP tool in customer visits, with the salesperson increasingly taking the lead during the calls. In doing so, the salesperson gains confidence and comfort in his or her ability to use the DSP tool through firsthand field experience. There is also ample chance, while driving around and during the social time in the evenings, for the area value champion and salesperson to build a relationship, making the salesperson feel comfortable calling the area value champion with any DSP questions or concerns that he or she may have.

Intergraph has put together résumés for its software offerings for engineering, procurement, and construction (EPC) firms and for plant owner-operators; these brochures describe the applications and benefits of the software, supported by a mix of named and disguised value case histories. Intergraph management wants its salespeople to use these résumés as value-based sales tools to demonstrate to EPC firms how they can make money by using the software and to demonstrate to plant owner-operators the cost savings they will realize in twelve months or less. The salespeople are trained on the value propositions and how to relate them to prospective customers.

To help salespeople understand how to persuasively convey the value proposition and to sell using the résumé tools, though, Frank Joop, Intergraph's executive director of global business development, will do joint sales calls with them. A recent example illustrates how such support generated success for a salesperson. The Middle East is one of Intergraphs's target markets for growth, and an influential prospective customer there was Aramco Services Company. Joop worked with the local salesperson on the presentation for Aramco, showing him how to position on the value of the offering rather than on selling the technology itself. They then made the presentation jointly, during which Joop modeled the desired statements about the value proposition and responses to questions for the salesperson. Working together, they closed this business and got Aramco to serve as a reference customer. This led to more business in the region with Sabic. Joop believes that working alongside the salesperson to make the presentation and close the business is the best way to persuade him or her to sell on value and use the value-based sales tools that Intergraph has developed.

Maintain comfort with selling value to customers. As we mentioned earlier, to ensure that salespeople continue to practice value-selling skills, suppliers may have a behavioral component as well as a profitable outcome component to their sales compensation plans. This compensation becomes part of the motivation for salespeople to demonstrate that they regularly use their value-based sales tools with customers and continue to build their proficiency and comfort with the tools. SKF and Rockwell Automation, among others, do this. We emphasize, though, that this behavioral component is only part of a salesperson's motivation.

Apart from this performance review and reward requirement, Rockwell's sales engineers want to continue to use the TCO Toolbox because they are convinced that it actually reduces the time to make a sale. As a couple of Rockwell sales engineers explained:

To us, the advantage of using TCO Toolbox is that it takes less time in the long run. It is true that it takes time to learn how to conduct a TCO analysis. It also takes time to collect the data and to input it into a model, particularly when the customer doesn't have it readily available or is reluctant to give it to us. Using a good TCO tool takes overall less time to close a sale than with the standard "feature and benefit" selling. In fact, the traditional approach has a significantly longer sales cycle. For example, it might take three or four sales calls spread out over several months to gain a sale. The TCO analysis takes a shorter [amount of] time. It also allows us to show where the cost savings originate. We gain credibility from it. Finally, once customers see numbers from TCO Toolbox, and what insights it can provide, they become willing to share more data.[3]

Suppliers that make value-based sales tools an integral part of their salespeople's everyday selling activities not only keep their value merchants from becoming value spendthrifts but continue to strengthen the sales force's value-selling capability. Applied Industrial Technologies, a leading reseller of bearings and other industrial supplies, furnishes an illustrative example. The foundation of Applied's selling efforts is its Documented Value Added (DVA) program. It requires every salesperson to record all their efforts to provide value for individual customers on a proprietary software package, which they access through Applied's intranet. Once they have provided the value, they must write up and record a DVA report. The DVA report summarizes what the salesperson did for the customer and estimates the cost savings that Applied has provided. The salesperson then presents the reports to customers at the end of the year. It's important to note that customer managers must sign off on the reports, acknowledging that the value Applied claims to have provided has, in fact, been provided. Since its inception, the DVA program has documented the provision of over $1 billion in savings for Applied customers!

Applied's salespeople use DVA as an integral part of their everyday selling activities in a number of ways. They use DVA reports to build customer loyalty and gain future sales. DVA enables the salesperson to say things like this: "Last year you purchased

$200,000 worth of MRO items from us. By doing so, you gained over $85,000 in documented cost savings from Applied." Applied's salespeople report that this not only takes the sting out of a 3–4 percent price increase, but it also enables them to gain the sale even when a competitor undercuts them on a price quote. Applied's salespeople also know that their customers' purchasing managers have to meet incentive goals. By providing documentation to these purchasing managers, Applied's salespeople help them effectively show their own managers that they have met their firm's cost reduction goals. Applied's salespeople help them earn their incentives.

The DVA reports also assist the Applied salesperson in targeting and acquiring new customers. The salesperson can sort DVA reports by customer firm, location, and industry. He or she can evaluate DVA reports across all the locations and divisions of a specific customer company and determine whether they can be replicated at that customer's other sites. This enables the salesperson to visit management at those sites and say, "We are doing X for your company at these other locations. Here's a DVA report that documents how much we saved them. We can do the same thing for you." The salesperson can also aggregate the reports across industries and assess patterns. He or she can then go to a prospective customer in that industry and offer to provide the same savings.

As this example from Applied amply illustrates, documenting the actual value provided to customers enables customer managers and the supplier to get credit for the superior value of its offerings. While this is worthwhile in itself, businesses that are value merchants make other use of this knowledge. By tracking the value that various customers are receiving from the company's offerings and performing some basic analyses, value merchants such as Applied gain a more fine-grained understanding of how the value of its offerings varies in terms of application, customer capabilities, and usage situation. Salespeople then leverage these insights to identify and prioritize prospects. Time is a scarce resource for salespeople, and they appreciate results-driven guidance that enables them to get the best return for themselves and for the firm. And sales force management can use the updated database to refine and extend the segmentation scheme used. When salespeople can see how their collective efforts to demonstrate and document superior value make their subsequent selling tasks easier and more productive, they want to use their value-based sales tools even more.

Finally, suppliers intent on transforming their salespeople into value merchants often develop a small number of value specialists, such as SKF's area value champions, to not only help the sales force understand the logic of customer value management and build its competence in the process and tools but to act as consultants who perform extraordinary customer value assessments. Most often, Rockwell Automation's sales engineers conduct TCO analyses that are limited in scope, focusing on the areas of most interest or concern to the customer to demonstrate Rockwell's points of difference in those areas. These analyses really do not drill down into *all* the costs and steps in the customer's entire production process; they focus on all the key activities of a particular application. If the customer requires or asks for a more extensive TCO analysis, the sales engineer calls in a TCO consultant from Rockwell's internal consulting group. When consultants come in to do the extensive, detailed TCO analysis, they charge a fee, which is either paid by the customer or jointly charged to Rockwell's sales and product marketing.

Instill and Invigorate a Value Merchant Culture

Businesses that want their salespeople to act as value merchants instill and invigorate a value merchant culture. Just as salespeople can be thought of as value merchants, so too can the businesses for which they work. These businesses adopt a philosophy of doing business based on demonstrating and documenting superior value to target customers. They bring this philosophy and culture to life through the processes and tools that we have been discussing. Yet senior management must take a broader view of persuasively conveying this value merchant mind-set and culture to everyone working in the business and to the customers. Salespeople's titles and designations, marketing communications, and what the business chooses to celebrate are each areas to express and invigorate a value merchant culture.

Emphasize a value merchant culture in salesperson titles. A salesperson's title has a subtle, yet profound effect on how the individual thinks about him- or herself. It also communicates to customers the way a business thinks about itself and its salespeople. Some progressive suppliers have recognized this and use it to instill and invigorate a value merchant culture. Consider the cases of Grainger and PeopleFlo Manufacturing.

After researching a number of potential value drivers, Grainger concluded that it was uniquely positioned to assist its customers in better managing their unplanned and infrequent purchases of maintenance, repair, and operating (MRO) supplies, which can account for a disproportionate amount of the typical customer's purchasing budget. The company, therefore, built a value proposition, which it terms the "Grainger value advantage," that assists customers in aggregating and consolidating infrequent and unplanned orders of MRO items, thus significantly reducing their total costs for MRO supplies. By serving as a one-stop shop for customers' unplanned MRO items, Grainger eliminates the need for its customers to hold excess inventory of rarely used items. Grainger further helps customer productivity by reducing the process cost of procuring hard-to-find products. It then designed a value-selling process and value-based sales tools to enable its sales force to deliver and substantiate this value proposition with customers. As part of this, it created the designation "certified value seller" to provide distinctive status and prestige to salespeople who demonstrate competence.

To become a certified value seller, a salesperson first attends the four-day Grainger value advantage boot camp, in which they learn and practice value-selling skills. Two weeks after the course, each salesperson must return with a polished value proposition for one of his or her customers, which the salesperson presents to a panel of sales managers. The salesperson must demonstrate that he or she is knowledgeable about Grainger's value proposition, is able to relate it to a customer's business issues to construct a compelling value proposition, and can put together evidence to support that value proposition. The sales managers throw out objections and challenge aspects of the value proposition, which the salesperson must handle. If the sales managers judge that the salesperson passes, he or she is certified as a value seller. If not, the salesperson must repeat the boot camp. By making this process rigorous, Grainger management signals that the firm intends to become a value merchant and that it means something to be a certified value seller.

PeopleFlo Manufacturing has committed itself, since its inception, to doing business based on demonstrating and documenting the superior value of its pumps to customers and getting a fair return. Its customers, which include some of the largest and most well-respected names in the process industry, are determined to reduce pump costs. They value a systematic approach to problem solving and a fact-based approach to evaluating life-cycle costs of pump alternatives. One visible sign of senior management's commitment to a value merchant philosophy and culture at PeopleFlo is the title of its salespeople: customer value manager. This title conveys what customers can expect from PeopleFlo's salespeople, which is to work consultatively with the customers to help them calculate the value, or operating cost savings, of PeopleFlo pump systems relative to the next-best alternative; justify a capital investment or maintenance expense; or share the ROI results with their colleagues.

Tout superior value in marketing communications. Businesses that act as value merchants tout the superior value of their offerings in marketing communications. Emphasizing how the firm delivers superior value frames customer expectations about doing business with the supplier, and it lays the foundation for subsequent sales calls. These marketing communications might be promotional pieces, advertisements, or articles written by supplier personnel. Applied Industrial Technologies, for example, used a series of case histories in advertisements appearing in industry publications to reinforce and make its value proposition tangible: "Award-winning service through documented value-added savings."

When the delivery of superior value to customers is highly technical, businesses acting as value merchants communicate this superior value in academic forums. The high-purity metal organics (HPMO) business of Akzo Nobel recently innovated a patented redesign of the cylinder for delivering its chemicals. The global sales and marketing manager presented papers on this new system at technical conferences and published articles on it in the top academic journals, such as the *IEEE Journal of Crystal Growth*. Prospective customers became aware of what Akzo Nobel was doing through these conference presentations and articles, which the company subsequently posted on its Web site, and called Akzo Nobel's salespeople.

Suppliers also can publish articles in industry publications to give customers greater knowledge of how they incur costs in their operations. In these articles supplier experts can draw on customer value research to specify cost drivers and the equations for customers to calculate previously not-well-understood costs. Sonoco's industrial products division has designed innovative winder tubes that enable superior string-up and transfer of fibers in fiber plants. In an article published in the *International Fiber Journal*, two Sonoco authors provided a summary table with waste categories, word equations, and a representative case example, which we present in table 6-1.

Recognize and reward extraordinary value merchants. Contests are one means of emphasizing and celebrating a value merchant culture. Setting the rules for the contest, determining who in the business is eligible to compete, and deciding how to celebrate, recognize, and reward top performers gives management

TABLE 6-1

Sonoco's string-up/transfer efficiency cost matrix

Waste category	Calculation	Example
Yarn waste	Divide the string-up time by 60 to change to hours, and multiply that number by the cost per pound and the throughput per hour.	$(12/60) \times (1.35 \times 60) = \$16.20$
Labor cost	Divide the string-up time by 60 to change to hours, and multiply that number by the number of operators and the labor cost per hour.	$(12/60) \times (2 \times \$22.00) = \$8.80$
Opportunity cost (additional production)	Divide the string-up time by 60 to change to hours, and multiply that number by the cost per pound and the throughput per hour.	$(12/60) \times (\$1.35 \times 60) = \$16.20$
Material cost	Multiply the number of tubes per winder by the cost per tube.	$4 \times \$1.00 = \$4.00$
Waste fiber cost (or revenue)	Multiply the fiber waste value per pound by the amount of pounds generated during each downtime, and subtract all costs associated with its disposal.	$(.15 \times 12) - (12 \times .02) = -\$1.56$
Total cost per failure	Add up all the above.	$\$43.64$
Cost of failure per day	Multiply the total cost per failure by the number of failures per day.	$\$43.64 \times 32 = \$1,396.48$
TOTAL ANNUAL COST	Multiply the cost of failure per day by the number of production days per year.	$\$1,396.48 \times 350 = \$488,768$

Source: Adapted from "Sonoco: Calculating the Costs of Yarn String-UP and Transfer Failures," *International Fiber Journal*, October 2005. Used with permission.

the chance to build and invigorate a value merchant culture throughout the business. In designing these contests, management should build on past success but strive each time to do something creative that adds a spark to the proceedings as well as further advances the business's value merchant culture.

Coinciding with the implementation of its Grainger value advantage market strategy in 2005, Grainger sponsored the Grainger value advantage contest for its entire sales force. At each district level, around ten local salespeople competed against one another to present the best value proposition. There were four criteria for judging the best value proposition:

1. How well did the salesperson persuasively communicate the Grainger value advantage story?

2. How well did the salesperson tailor the value proposition to the customer's business issues?

3. How compelling was the salesperson's proposed solution?

4. How well was the salesperson able to handle questions and objections on the value proposition?

Winners at the district level then competed at the regional level. In turn, the regional winner competed at the national level. Four national winners were then invited to present their value propositions at Grainger's national sales and service meeting in Orlando in March 2006. There, they had to get up onstage in front of over three thousand sales and service personnel and present their value propositions to a panel of sales and marketing managers. The panelists challenged each salesperson on his or her value proposition. As the presentations began, Grainger's president, James Ryan, appeared unexpectedly and joined the panel. The crowd went wild. Ryan assumed the role of the customer and challenged every value proposition. He grilled each presenter, asking tough questions. The contest served to recognize and reward Grainger's extraordinarily skilled salespersons. Three of the four presenters subsequently were promoted.

When a business uses resellers to reach the market, how can it convey a value merchant mind-set to its resellers' salespeople? Swagelok—a supplier of advanced and innovative fluid system products, services, and solutions to a wide range of global industries—provides an instructive case. Swagelok trains its resellers' salespeople on value selling, making use of its value impact program (VIP) reports, which document the actual savings that the customer has received from Swagelok offerings. Salespeople prepare VIP reports for each of their key accounts and "customers of impact" and provide those reports to both customers and Swagelok. Through this, knowledge of how Swagelok's offerings deliver superior value to customers is updated and expanded.

To promote a value merchant mind-set among its resellers, Swagelok complements its reseller compensation with recognition, in the form of Swagelok's annual sales activity contest. All Swagelok resellers—both in the United States and in other countries—participate. One of the chief categories in the contest is the average number of VIP reports per salesperson. On its intranet, Swagelok has created a leader board (like in a golf tournament). Leading resellers in each region are reported per category as well as their point totals.

At a special awards dinner during its annual global sales meeting, Swagelok senior management presents gold, silver, and bronze awards and plaques of recognition to the top three reseller businesses in terms of average number of VIP reports per salesperson. Note that the awards recognize the reseller business and its salespeople for being extraordinary value merchants. Interestingly, no monetary award is presented—just recognition. However, this recognition is coveted by Swagelok resellers and promotes healthy and friendly competition among them. Reportedly, one reseller senior manager who recently received the gold award told Swagelok's vice president of marketing: "This award is worth more than $10,000 to me!"

Composites One invigorates and celebrates a value merchant culture among its business units and salespeople with the annual Margin Builder Award Contest. It has thirty distribution centers throughout the United States, each of which is a profit center with salespeople. Distribution centers (DCs) as well as salespeople compete in this contest because DC workers can affect gross margin dollars, too. Customer service personnel located at a DC, for example, review orders and remind customers to purchase items that they may have neglected to order. "Margin builder scores" are the sum of the percentage increase in total gross margin dollars and the percentage increase in gross margin (expressed as a percentage). Each month during the year, everyone working at Composites One receives the *Margin Builder News*, which recounts recent accomplishments of salespeople and DCs in margin building and lists the top ten DCs and top ten sales representatives, with their margin builder scores (July 2006's headline was "Margin Builder Race Set Off Fireworks of Its Own!"). At the end of the year, everyone receives the final results, recognizing the winning DCs and sales representatives (the final headline of 2006 was "Victory!").

One DC is the annual Margin Builder Award Contest winner, and there is also a regional winner in each of the other three regions. Everyone working at the overall winning DC receives a $100 gift certificate. The overall winner and three regional winner DCs each receive an engraved plaque to display and have lunch brought in for everyone twice per month for the entire year.

The sales representative who is the annual Margin Builder Award Contest grand prize winner receives an all-expenses-paid trip for two to a location of his or her choice. The sales representatives that finish second and third each receive gift certificates. Perhaps more desired, though, is the social recognition that they receive. The three winning sales representatives are invited, with their significant others, to a special presentation event at corporate headquarters, where they receive an engraved plaque and are made lifelong members of the president's club. Members of the president's club each receive a very nice, subtle blue sports jacket. At each national sales meeting, there is one event or reception where the members of the president's club (present and past winners) wear these sports jackets and are recognized by their peers and Composites One management.

How Milliken Transformed Its Sales Force into Value Merchants

As an outstanding case study in transforming field salespeople into value merchants, consider Milliken, one of the largest privately held textile, carpet, and chemical manufacturers in the world. In 1999, like many U.S. manufacturing firms, Milliken found some market segments under intensifying price pressure as imports increased and supply chains gradually shifted toward low-wage countries. Customer satisfaction had declined, and a significant amount of the company's sales revenue was threatened. In addition, some of Milliken's older product offerings had become more and more vulnerable due to limited intellectual property protection.

Milliken's management recognized that competing with the low-cost competitors only on price would be difficult, given that Milliken did not always have the lowest structural cost position in the market. Therefore, the company needed to find new ways to create superior value beyond its products or run the risk of sales and profit erosion due to low-cost competition. To accomplish this, Milliken began a customer value engineering (CVE) initiative, which was launched in the performance products division. This CVE initiative was driven by a cross-functional team composed of the division president, business development manager, division director of strategy and marketing, three market managers, and the product market management improvement leader. The market managers were instrumental in incorporating sales force insights from their respective markets. Together, they conducted a sales and market manager survey, which showed that "operational excellence" and "innovation" were most valuable to Milliken's customers. Building on this insight, the CVE team began to develop a detailed value calculator tool, which identified potential favorable points of difference and quantified their financial value (monetary cost savings or revenue gained) from the customer's perspective. The value calculator tool evaluated Milliken along six performance areas: product consistency, product convenience, product customization, service consistency, service convenience, and service customization. Each dimension was further broken down into key performance facets.

Based on these research findings, the CVE team launched a campaign called "Working Together, Winning Together," which highlighted three primary benefits for customers: continuous improvement/operational excellence, innovation and new product leadership, and world-class service. The team members developed an accompanying value-selling and delivery process. They put together a value presentation tool to assist the sales force with developing creative solutions that add value while generating higher margin dollars per customer.

A noteworthy success from this campaign comes from Milliken's work with a large consumer products company, which needed to reduce its total costs in its core business. Milliken's relationship with the company was new but growing. The customer came to Milliken looking for new technology for a specific textile product. Milliken assembled a cross-functional team, which worked with the customer on developing new technology options to help it reduce its total costs. Out of numerous identified opportunities for improvement, Milliken and the customer jointly developed, tested, and validated several solutions to penetrate the customer's target market. By setting up tangible customer metrics—such as total processing costs, cost of defects, and unpacking costs—they were able to evaluate the various solutions. Results were impressive. The customer achieved cumulative savings of $7 million within three years (greater than 7 percent of total cost savings) and improved quality (from 2.4 percent off quality to 0.8 percent). The customer was so satisfied with Milliken that it chose to purchase 100 percent of its products from the company.

By providing its salespeople with CVE tools, Milliken has been able to empower them to develop innovative value propositions to suit customers' unique business requirements. The sales force is extensively trained on the value-selling process in four areas: investigating customer requirements and preferences, demonstrating value, negotiating terms and conditions, and driving results. Salespeople are evaluated and rewarded based on their businesses' margin dollar growth, which guards them against the temptation of price cuts and short-term spikes in volume. Further, they have personal incentives for CVE participation as well as mandated bi-annual CVE reviews with the president of the division. The sales managers also periodically meet with customers to review business performance. All these systems and processes instill a sense of ownership for customer value management in the sales force.

The CVE team is actively promoting the value-based marketing philosophy within the company. Most salespeople have seen the value of CVE and embrace it. However, some salespeople who have been in the company for over twenty-five years have moved slowly, saying that they know their customers and what will work. In terms of adoption, one-third of salespeople use CVE all the time, one-third use it for their more significant customers, and the remaining one-third do so only when they have to present to upper management. The CVE team recognizes this and is introducing several initiatives to create visibility for CVE in the division and the company. An intranet site showcasing CVE best practices and success stories provides salespeople with an incentive to adopt and deliver on the value-based approach. Presentations at division meetings and peer feedback serve as powerful mechanisms for knowledge sharing and learning within the organization. Success stories are documented and repeatedly reinforced in sales and division meetings. These various initiatives have generated significant momentum for CVE across the organization. Milliken plans to roll it out to thirty-four of its top fifty customers in the performance products division. These top fifty customers account for two-thirds of revenue and 135 percent of division growth.

Communicating its superior value to customers has become critical for Milliken to retain and grow its existing customers as well as defend and maintain its price premiums. In a span of five years, Milliken has registered record revenue growth, largely driven by share gain versus competitors, and a significant increase in operating profits. By empowering the sales force to become value merchants, Milliken has not only etched a powerful position for itself in the marketplace but also fundamentally transformed itself from a traditional engineering company to a truly customer-focused company.

SEVEN

Profit from Value Provided

Earning an Equitable Return

Throughout this book, we have argued that suppliers must deliver superior value to their target customers compared to the next-best alternative. Yet, as challenging as this is for them to do consistently, most find it still more challenging to get an equitable or fair return on the value they provide. Understanding, creating, and delivering superior value often requires larger investments and greater resources from the supplier. And even when this is not the case, providing superior value compared to the next-best alternative means that it is reasonable for a supplier to expect something more in return from the customers it serves.

In today's competitive business markets, though, profiting from superior value does not happen as a natural consequence of providing it. Suppliers must invest in developing the mind-set, the processes, and the systems that will enable them to earn an equitable return. Thus, suppliers that are value merchants are mindful of and stress both aspects of success in business markets—delivering superior value compared to the next-best alternative *and* obtaining an equitable return for the value provided.

Suppliers must first understand and then exploit the different ways in which to obtain a fair return from customers. They also should manage pricing as if profitability depended on it. After we consider each of these points, we present the instructive case of how Siam City Cement profited from providing superior value.

Obtain a Fair Return on Superior Value

The first thought most supplier managers have about how they can profit from superior value is by asking for, and getting, a price premium vis-à-vis the next-best alternative. When first considered, this does seem fair. If the supplier provides value to the customer beyond the next-best alternative, it should be able to command a higher price. And, indeed, obtaining a price premium for the firm's products or services compared to its competitors is an obvious way to profit from the value provided.

Unfortunately, in many hypercompetitive business markets, getting a price premium is rather difficult. Thus, it is critical for suppliers to understand and exploit all the potential means for getting a fair return. We can understand the possibilities by decomposing customer contribution to profitability, as depicted in figure 7-1. Customer contribution to profitability has two fundamental components: willingness to pay and cost to serve. A supplier can attempt to improve a customer's willingness to pay for its market offerings, or it can attempt to lower the cost to serve that customer.

Each of these fundamental components can be further partitioned into two constituent elements or potential sources of incremental profit. "Willingness to pay" can be divided into "price premiums" and a "more profitable mix of business." The latter element refers to those situations in which certain offerings in the

FIGURE 7-1

Getting a fair return on superior value provided to customers

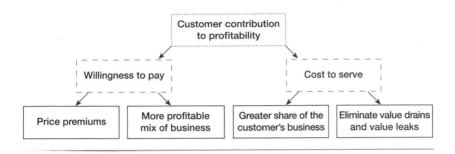

set purchased by the customer substantially increase that customer's profitability to the supplier. "Cost to serve" can be broken down into "greater share of the customer's business" and "eliminating value drains and leaks." *Greater share of the customer's business* refers to the share of the customer's purchase requirements for market offerings like those that the supplier is presently providing, whereas *mix of business* refers to a supplier's share of the customer's total purchase requirements for all product offerings that the supplier would be able to, and would prefer to, supply. *Value drains* are services, programs, and systems that cost the supplier more to provide than they are worth to customers and that have no strategic significance. *Value leaks* are those customer activities and practices that increase the cost of doing business for the customer and/or the supplier and that yield no offsetting greater cost savings or value to either.

We encourage you to think about which of these your business pursues to gain profit from superior value. As we discuss each of these means of getting a fair return, consider whether your firm has adequately explored and exploited it. Our intent is to convey how suppliers have successfully pursued each of these to improve customer contribution to profitability and, by extension, how you might also.

Gaining a Price Premium

When a supplier's offering delivers demonstrably superior value to that of the next-best alternative, seeking a price premium over the price of the next-best alternative should be its initial approach. This is especially the case when the source of this superior value is patent-protected intellectual property. Seeking and gaining a price premium establishes a reference point in the minds of customers of what the supplier believes is a fair exchange. It also encourages competitors that will try to emulate the supplier to also seek a price premium for their offerings.

Sonoco gains a price premium for its Sonotube forms. Sonoco's industrial products division has sold Sonotube concrete forms for years. These forms, made of paper and fiber, are used in light commercial and residential applications. Concrete is poured into them, and after the concrete cures, the tube material is stripped off. Over the years, the product's differentiation faded to the point that Sonoco was making 70 percent of its Sonotube forms under private label for distributors and only 30 percent under its own brand. One problem with the original Sonotube was its lack of resistance to water. Inclement weather prohibited the use of the paper/fiber concrete forms. Through research it conducted, Sonoco uncovered that some customers required water resistance. And Sonoco was able to innovate and create a water-resistant form, which it branded as "Sonotube forms with RainGuard technology."

Sonotube with RainGuard technology significantly reduces the risk of blowouts—that is, when a generic fiber form fails after becoming saturated by water or rain. The pH of concrete is very high, which, with water, deteriorates the adhesive holding the tube together. Sonoco has done calculations on the cost of a blowout to demonstrate the cost savings to concrete contractors. The company's salespeople have worksheets—a value-based sales tool—that they can use to quantify the costs of a blowout to a contractor. They stress that such analyses must be based on facts.

This new, improved product has been a resounding success. Sonotube with RainGuard technology has received up to a 20 percent price premium over competing generic forms and about a 5 percent price premium over previous Sonotube forms, and the company has seen a 16 percent increase in sales. Sonoco also was able to use this new technology to reconnect users with the Sonotube brand and its distinct value versus generic, and often inferior-performing, private-label forms. Sonoco was able to halt the slow deterioration of the Sonotube brand, which was being used generically to describe fiber concrete column forms, and to stop producing the private-label forms and convert all of this business back to the branded Sonotube with RainGuard technology product.

SKF links price premiums to product performance. As suppliers gain experience in documenting the actual value provided to customers, they become knowledgeable about how their offerings deliver superior value to customers and even how the actual value delivered varies across different kinds of customers. Because of this extensive and detailed knowledge, they become confident in predicting the cost savings and added value that prospective customers will likely receive. Some value merchant businesses have become so accurate in these predictions that they are willing to make their price premiums contingent on performance, payable after documenting savings to customers.

SKF leverages the knowledge it gains from its Documented Solution Program tool to secure performance-based contracts with customers. These contracts are structured as risk-sharing, gain-sharing agreements for which SKF offers an integrated maintenance service package. The company is paid for documented results in meeting mutually defined key performance indexes. SKF even offers flexibility on how it is paid. The customer may pay only a portion of the fee up front, with the remaining portion paid as performance targets are met. Alternatively, the customer may pay by awarding SKF a larger share of its business over time. We reproduce a recent SKF ad in figure 7-2 that touts the company's willingness to share risk, not just profit, with customers.

Improving the Mix of Customer Business

A supplier can also profit from receiving a better (i.e., more profitable) mix of business from the customer. The same amount of dollar sales to a customer may have very different profit implications based on the mix of products and services sold or on the customer locations served. It is well known that having a customer source higher-margin products or services helps improve the supplier's profitability. In fact, most cross-selling programs are based on this approach. Yet most suppliers have not methodically thought this through or pursued a well-defined strategy over time to profitably grow their mix of business. In contrast, consider the refreshing example of Keppel Seghers's better technology group.

Seghers pursues a more profitable mix of business. Seghers is a Belgium-based design, engineering, fabrication, and maintenance company that serves the petrochemical, power generation, food-processing, and water treatments industries worldwide.[1] Because it must leverage limited resources, Seghers has devised and honed a growth strategy that pivots on the progressive expansion of its relationship with its customers to gain the most profitable mix of those customers' business. This strategy capitalizes on increasing customer demands for one-stop shopping for industrial services and on a trend toward outsourcing plant maintenance, and it features a sequence of four business development steps.

In pursuing initial business with targeted accounts, Seghers focuses on providing one special service or activity for which it has a distinctive capability, such as bolt tensioning, on-site machining, or valve repair and overhaul. Seghers makes a concerted effort to furnish outstanding service during the initial encounter to build customer confidence in its capabilities.

FIGURE 7-2

SKF Reliability Systems advertisement: Sharing risk, not just savings

Most companies are happy to share profit.
SKF Reliability Systems is willing to

share risk.

An alternative to traditional maintenance practices or full outsourcing, an Integrated Maintenance Solution (IMS) gives SKF Reliability Systems responsibility for your machine asset management strategy. We share some of the risk as well as the savings, while you receive agreed upon financial returns and technology upgrades—without capital investment.

Our on-site team provides the services and support best suited to optimize your plant's asset efficiency and integrity. All services are delivered under one fixed-fee, performance-based contract. Also included in the terms is a guarantee that SKF will pay back part of the contracted fee if agreed upon goals are not met.

Each agreement is different, customized to your specific business needs, complementing your internal resources.

Is an IMS agreement right for you? Contact us to discuss your potential ROI, and to hear some of the results we've produced for other companies.

SKF USA Inc
www.skfusa.com

SKF.

Source: Provided courtesy of SKF USA Inc. Used with permission.

It then builds on this experience to propose a second level of service that it could profitably provide—ongoing plant maintenance. Again, it is important to note that Seghers does *not* pursue all maintenance business within a plant or refinery. Instead, it pursues just those services for which it has distinctive capabilities and that would yield significant profits. And when the customer insists on a total maintenance solution, Seghers selectively partners with another contractor that provides the required complementary services. Seghers's senior management finds ongoing maintenance service to be a golden opportunity to gain in-depth knowledge of a customer's requirements. In fact, Seghers's technicians are trained to spot and report on any service opportunities.

Major equipment overhaul serves as the third step in Seghers's account growth strategy. For example, overhauling heat exchangers is a complicated and difficult operation for a customer's maintenance staff to perform, yet it is a rather profitable service for Seghers. Such an overhaul may take several days to complete and may involve a team of Seghers's technicians and costly machining equipment and instrumentation.

When the customer becomes fully confident in the company's capabilities, Seghers's sales managers pursue the fourth level of desired business—total shutdown service. Seghers provides two forms: planned and emergency shutdown. Total shutdown service is its most elaborate one. It includes piping repair and replacement, valve and pump overhaul, vessel overhaul and replacement, and control system maintenance. The work is expensive and may require an entire refinery to shut down for a week or more. For Seghers, this turns out to be demanding and yet much more profitable work.

Sonoco finds profitable new business with present customers. Supplier salespeople can dramatically improve the profitability of a customer account by finding profitable business for other units of their firm. While every supplier would like this to happen, few have made any concerted effort in programs and incentives to methodically accomplish it. What would such an effort look like?

Sonoco has a growth readiness program, which has a goal of double-digit profitable, sustainable growth each year. To lead and monitor the progress of this program, Sonoco has created a growth council, which is composed of the heads of the commercial organizations for each of the Sonoco business units (twelve in total). A recent initiative the growth council sponsored was the Universal Sonoco Night (USN) program. This initiative was aimed at motivating greater selling across Sonoco business units. Each USN lasted an afternoon, an evening, and the following morning. Eddie Smith, corporate vice president of strategy and business development, and other members of the growth council attended six USNs, which were held in each geographic region of the United States. Ninety percent of Sonoco salespeople attended a USN. At night, there was a trade fair, where representatives from each of the business units provided salespeople with basic knowledge of their business unit and sufficient information about their products.

Each salesperson also received a "blueprint," which was a document that detailed a process on how to identify a customer's need for other Sonoco products and, when a potential opportunity emerged, on how to forward the gathered information to the designated point person at the appropriate business unit. This point person served as the primary contact and evaluated the information to determine whether to send in a product expert along with the salesperson to begin the cross-selling or solution-selling process. During the USNs, Sonoco senior management addressed a potential salesperson concern: "Why should I put my relationship with the customer at risk to leverage other potential Sonoco business?" Smith stressed that leveraging the Sonoco portfolio of products to provide solutions deepens the relationship with the customer, so rather than creating risk, it strengthens customer relations.

The growth council also provided an enticing financial incentive. If a salesperson went through a joint selling process with the product expert and was successful, he or she would earn 1 percent

of the first twelve months of sales revenue for the realized opportunity—up to 50 percent of his or her annual incentive plan. An
interesting aspect was that a salesperson could close an unlimited
number of such opportunities, earning up to 50 percent of his or
her annual incentive plan from each realized opportunity. These
across-division incentive awards were in addition to any earnings
from the salesperson's regular incentive plan and were not subject
to any division pool limitations. Finally, if a salesperson was able
to close the sale for another business unit without the assistance
of a product expert in that unit (e.g., if an adhesives salesperson
closed business for selling paperboard), he or she would earn 2
percent of the first twelve months of sales revenue—again, up to
50 percent of the annual target bonus from the incentive plan.
Early results suggest that this initiative will be a great success.

Building the Share of Customer Business

Improving the mix of business makes the most of the customer's
willingness to pay by selling it other offerings that it's not as price
sensitive about and that have better margins than what it is presently
purchasing from the supplier. In contrast, building the share of the
customer's business focuses on the cost to serve the customer by
fulfilling a greater proportion of its requirements, thereby reducing the total cost per unit supplied. A supplier must gain an estimate
of the percentage of each customer's total purchase requirements
for each market offering that the supplier provides. Although most
firms in business markets have some estimate of their market share,
much fewer have estimates of their share of each customer's business in the markets they serve. Yet the share of the customer's
business is a better diagnostic because it pinpoints customer accounts
that perceive the supplier's offering as superior to those of competitors and suggests sources of differentiation.

Suppose that a supplier has a 20 percent market share. It is
unlikely that each customer in the market is purchasing 20 percent
of its requirements from the supplier. Rather, some customers

purchase nothing from the supplier, and others purchase more than 20 percent of their requirements from the supplier. What differentiates large-share customers from minor-share customers, and what sources of differentiation are possible if the customer were to give the supplier 100 percent share?

When the customer has multiple locations, further insight comes from understanding how the supplier's business is spread across locations. Thus, if a customer has ten plants in its manufacturing network, what percentage of each plant's purchase requirements does each of the supplier's offerings account for? A supplier may find that the percentage of a given offering varies dramatically across customer locations, from being the single source to supplying nothing at all. The cost to serve a customer and the customer's own total cost of ownership can vary significantly, depending on how the same amount of supplier business is spread across locations.

Multiple single sourcing is a concept that enables customers and suppliers to reap the benefits of single source arrangements while minimizing the potential drawbacks. Under a multiple single sourcing arrangement, each plant in a customer's manufacturing network is single sourced, yet the customer maintains at least two suppliers across the network. For example, a customer with ten manufacturing plants would have one single-source supplier at six of its plants and another single-source supplier at the other four plants, with each supplier serving as the backup to the other. As part of the arrangement, the customer might require each supplier to share process or product improvements with the other. The customer could then keep track of the improvements each supplier contributed and use that as a criterion for awarding future business.

Gaining a deep understanding of customers' requirements and preferences takes time and other resources. It is worthwhile only when the supplier receives a large share of their business. Yet best-practice suppliers pursue single sourcing for the business that is strategically right for them. Consider the experiences of Seghers and Milliken.

Seghers gains the targeted share of a customer's business. Seghers relies on account profitability analysis to guide its efforts at building shares of customers' business. It's important to note that the company avoids pursuing large sales revenue of marginally profitable business in favor of becoming a focused single-source provider of a customer's purchase requirements. A *focused single-source provider* attempts to attain 100 percent of a customer's business in targeted offering categories while not pursuing other categories that it could supply to that customer.

For example, one of Seghers's key accounts built a plant next to an existing plant on the same property. While most competitors have pursued service opportunities in the newer plant while shunning the older plant, Seghers has done the reverse. Why? Because the older plant has a far greater need for profitable maintenance services, and, knowing the older equipment well, Seghers has a distinctive capability to maintain it.

At the same time, Seghers's profit analyses have shown that the newer plant only requires low-margin services. Why? In part because it contains new state-of-the art equipment, which does not require a lot of maintenance and overhaul work. Worse still, there are a number of competitors that are capable of maintaining this equipment and lack the discipline to refrain from chasing low-price business. Through diligent efforts, Seghers has gained 100 percent of the business in the older plant while leaving the relatively unattractive business at the newer plant for competitors to battle over.

Milliken grows its share of a customer's business. In 2005, a large automotive supplier, to whom Milliken offered seating products, was losing market share and experiencing quality and delivery issues. Armed with Milliken's value calculator tool, the sales manager was able to creatively develop multiple solutions to help the automotive supplier reengineer its product, reduce its inventory, and achieve on-time delivery. Milliken initiated a joint team composed of key members of both organizations to better understand and prioritize the most important needs and to ensure shared accountability in value creation and capture.

The team developed a string of solutions. It developed detailed customer metrics, such as days of inventory held and on-time delivery, and monitored progress monthly to achieve results. These clear and transparent metrics also enabled the joint team to resolve conflicts. In five years, the solution reduced the customer's inventory by 66 percent and achieved five years of 100 percent on-time delivery. The customer's market share increased by 10 percent, and its total cost of ownership was reduced by more than 15 percent. The customer has been extremely satisfied with Milliken's new supply chain process. In return for the superior value Milliken has delivered to this customer, it has made Milliken its single-source supplier.

Eliminating Value Drains and Leaks

Identifying and eliminating value drains and leaks are a promising means for value merchants to improve their own, as well as their customers', profitability. These changes in how the supplier and customer do business can provide cost savings to each, or one may incur incremental cost while the other gains greater offsetting cost savings. In the latter case, most suppliers and customers are willing to share the net cost savings as an incentive to change, so that each firm is better off. Success at identifying and eliminating value drains and leaks promotes greater cooperation between a supplier and customer. Customer value assessment and activity-based costing analysis are the "Aha!" tools to detect value drains and leaks.

Eastman Chemical identifies and eliminates a value drain. Eastman Chemical—a leading producer of chemicals, plastics, and fibers—provides a notable example of identifying and eliminating a value drain. It was supplying an organic chemical intermediate to a leading pigment producer and was having difficulty getting to a price at which the customer would be happy to do business. The Eastman salesperson, who had been trained in selling value and doing customer-process mapping, proposed studying the customer's production process to discover potential cost savings. This investigation revealed a value drain. Eastman, in the final step of its production process, was eliminating moisture from this product, which was the traditional way of providing it to customers. The salesperson discovered that the first step in the customer's process was to add moisture back into the product!

When apprised of this value drain, Eastman changed its process to eliminate this step. The company was able to achieve efficiency increases in production as a result, creating a model that allowed other customers with similar process steps to be converted later. Eastman was able to improve its profitability while passing a portion of the savings on to the customer in the form of a smaller price increase.

Tata Steel identifies and eliminates value drains and leaks. Tata Steel is a leading supplier in India. Through its customer value management (CVM) process, it strives to find and eliminate value drains and leaks in doing business with its strategic customers. Since the launch of CVM, there has been a significant drop in costs across the value chain between Tata and these customers and a significant increase in business for Tata from these customers.

The relationship between these customers and Tata has undergone a notable change, from being adversarial to being mutually reinforcing. Often, once the relationship is cemented through the CVM process, the customer also begins to contribute ideas on potential value drains and leaks. This is a magical moment in the relationship. When this happens, an enlightened senior manager from the customer firm might ask, "Why is Tata losing money while trying to help us? Let us find ways that Tata can help us save money and at the same time make money for itself."

In a value drain example from the tubes business, Tata supplied steel tubes to a boiler manufacturer located a thousand miles away. The tubes, after manufacturing, were specially oiled to avoid rusting en route to the customer's plant. Bizarre as it may seem, the customer first cleaned the oiled surfaces and then treated them to pick up rust in its plant! As the CVM assessment revealed, a little bit of rust on the tubes was desirable to create enough friction between the tube and the bobbin drum while making coil-type boilers. Eliminating the oiling process at Tata and the subsequent cleaning process at the customer's end was a win-win solution for both firms. This has resulted in $30 to $40 of savings per metric ton for the customer while lowering Tata's costs by eliminating the oiling step in its process.

In a value leak example, Tata shipped large tonnages of steel bars in straight and fixed lengths of twelve meters to construction firms purchasing steel reinforcing bars. The customer wanted differential lengths of ten meters or eleven meters, but the fixed-length offering from Tata created a 12–16 percent loss for the customer. The relationship was an arm's-length transactional relationship. The CVM process revealed the value leaks to the Tata sales manager and the customer representative. The two firms decided that it was more appropriate to roll and cut customized lengths at the Tata factory and then ship the bars in ready to use lengths to the customer. Tata and its customer conducted an assessment of the extra costs that Tata would incur to make customized lengths at its mill and the cost savings in conversion and wastage that the customer would receive from customized lengths. The two firms then were able to arrive at a price premium for customized lengths that more than covered Tata's incremental costs while providing the greater portion of the cost savings to the customer. Tata finds that passing along the greater proportion of the identified cost savings delights the customer while still giving Tata a "good enough" incremental margin over its additional costs.

In 2002, before the start of CVM, the top sixteen customers accounted for just 15 percent of Tata's revenue in one of its business lines. In 2005, the revenue share from these sixteen customers had increased to 35 percent. The marked improvement in share was due to the higher share of business that these customers gave to Tata by diverting business from other suppliers and engaging Tata in developing new products, and due to the increase in these customers' overall requirements as a result of Tata's own growth in India. The end result is that Tata is more often supplying these customers higher-end and more-customized products that differentiate it from competitors while also providing a higher level of profitability.

Quaker Chemical identifies and eliminates value leaks. Quaker Chemical's fundamental strategy is to create a relationship with its customers that allows for the execution of projects that result in added value and benefit for both the company itself and the customer. A prominent way in which Quaker accomplishes this is through its chemical management program. A Quaker employee works at the customer's manufacturing facility and performs all the activities related to the chemical processes. By having Quaker personnel on-site, the customer gains added value in the areas of productivity, product quality, and reduced chemical usage and waste. A recent Quaker experience at a major steel company illustrates how it works to identify and eliminate value leaks.

The customer's five-stand rolling mill was accumulating $134,000 in total costs per year for product that did not meet specification, along with other quality problems in producing sheet steel. Trusting in Quaker's expertise, the customer proposed a collaborative approach to address this problem. Quaker's first step in the effort was creating customer awareness of both total process cost and the most recent advances in steel rolling. Quaker did this by sharing its knowledge on improved test methods, educating the customer on advanced principles of steel rolling from various research programs, and establishing a baseline total cost for the current cold rolling oil. The next step was to propose an upgrade in the quality of the cold rolling lubricants used to process the steel. The proposed upgrade was expected to solve the customer's problems of rust and pinholes in uncoated products—a value leak. It also was expected to improve other aspects of the rolling process, including productivity and cost reduction. Due to these expected improvements, the two companies modified their contract to determine how they would share in the anticipated results.

The revised contract provided for the steel company to pay Quaker on the basis of tons of steel produced. The steel company would receive 80 percent of the benefits produced, and Quaker would receive the other 20 percent. The contract also stipulated that the steel company would retain any value realized from the increase in the steel coil production rate. The fact that the contract covered a five-year span was unique to that customer but was necessary for both companies to commit the resources needed to improve performance over an extended period of time.

Over those five years, the upgrade project achieved almost 3 million "hard" dollars in quantifiable value, well in excess of the original expectations. In addition, a comparable amount of "soft" dollar value was created in key cost areas, including improvements in quality, process performance and utilization, labor requirements and maintenance, and mill cleanliness. These improvements included increasing throughput capacity by 2 percent, improving lubrication, reducing consumption of rolling oil lubricants by 35 percent, and eliminating the production of nonprime product (due to pinholes in uncoated products and rust problems). Iron particle generation during rolling also was reduced, resulting in reduced oil consumption without operational changes, thereby eliminating another value leak.

Despite a 35 percent decrease in the sale of rolling oil products, Quaker maintained its revenue at the original level. Why? Because Quaker was compensated on the tons of steel produced, rather than on the traditional method of product sales per gallon. Quaker actually received a 75 percent increase in the unit price for its rolling oil because the amount used by the customer was lower. This increase compensated Quaker for higher raw material costs and the amount of staff time and effort invested to achieve the process improvements. In addition to covering the increased costs, the payment terms provided Quaker with a 10 percent increase in gross margin. Thus, working together to identify and eliminate value leaks significantly improved profitability for Quaker and its customer.

Manage Pricing as if Profitability Depended on It

How do suppliers in business markets decide on a specific price for their market offerings? According to Hermann Simon, an expert on pricing, "In most firms prices are determined by intuition, opinions, rules of thumb, outright dogma, top management's higher wisdom, or internal power fights."[2] That quotation accurately captures our experience in business markets. Even though superior pricing capability has a significant impact on profitability, strangely enough, few suppliers in business markets attempt to systematically build and leverage their pricing capability.[3]

Although suppliers in business markets often base their prices simply on their own costs or the prices of competitors' offerings, value-based pricing is an alternative worth considering. Further, pricing consideration ought to take place at the strategic level, at the tactical level, and at the transactional level. Each of these can have a significant effect on profitability.

Value-Based Pricing

Our philosophy is that price should be set in relation to a market offering's value, which is called *value-based pricing*. Underpinning pricing is the fundamental value equation that we presented in chapter 2:

$$(\text{Value}_f - \text{Price}_f) > (\text{Value}_a - \text{Price}_a) \quad (\text{Eq. 7-1})$$

In that equation, Value_f and Price_f are the value and price of the firm's market offering (Offering$_f$), and Value_a and Price_a are the value and price of the next-best alternative (Offering$_a$). In practice, a rearrangement of this equation better captures how customer firm managers decide between offerings:

$$\Delta \text{Value}_{f,a} > (\text{Price}_f - \text{Price}_a) \quad \text{(Eq. 7-2)}$$

Often, value analyses or value assessments are performed on a comparative basis, where the differences in performance and total cost are ascertained for two market offerings of interest. These differences then are expressed in monetary terms and summed to obtain $\Delta \text{Value}_{f,a}$. Equation 7-2 also represents a natural way that customer managers decide between two offerings, answering this question: "What is the difference in the worth of the two offerings to my firm, and how does this compare to the difference in their prices?"

However, Value$_f$, Value$_a$, and Price$_a$ indicate nothing about a specific price that the firm should choose for Offering$_f$. We rearrange equation 7-2 to isolate Price$_f$ on the left side of the equation:

$$\text{Price}_f < \text{Price}_a + \Delta \text{Value}_{f,a} \quad \text{(Eq. 7-3)}$$

Given that Price$_a$ is known, which after some investigation is usually the case, equation 7-3 then defines the feasible range of prices the firm could charge and still maintain the inequality. Equation 7-3 also reveals an insight: that when $\Delta \text{Value}_{f,a}$ is either zero (the definition of a commodity) or unknown and therefore regarded as though it were zero, selling discussions with customers will be focused primarily on price. So we can see that competition-based pricing is actually a special case of value-based pricing, when either of these two situations are the case.

Pricing Strategy

Let us consider figure 7-3 to better understand value-based pricing strategy. Because value is expressed as the worth in monetary terms, we provide a value continuum expressed in Swiss francs per unit. For simplicity (but without loss of generality), we assume

FIGURE 7-3

Value-based pricing strategy

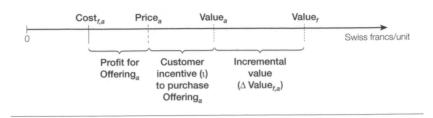

the cost of Offering$_f$ and Offering$_a$ are the same. The difference between Price$_a$ and Cost$_a$ defines the profit for Offering$_a$. The difference between Value$_a$ and Price$_a$ represents the customer incentive to purchase Offering$_a$. Note that in business markets, the value provided will likely exceed the price; otherwise, the customer won't be interested in the offering.

Now, the difference between Value$_f$ and Value$_a$ represents the incremental value Offering$_f$ provides over Offering$_a$. What part of this incremental value to retain as profit and what part to share with the customer as an incentive to purchase is a strategic decision. The business must decide on its market strategy for the market segment. That is, what does the business want to accomplish? "Sell more," by the way, is not a sufficiently well-developed market strategy. Wanting customers to change from purchasing an in-kind, upgraded offering to purchasing the next-generation offering, for example, might represent a market strategy.

Having decided on the market strategy, the business then chooses a *marketing* strategy to accomplish the market strategy, one element of which is the pricing strategy. Pricing strategy focuses on where within this range to position the market offering and how to shift the range itself and the supplier's relative position within it. It's significant to note that by sharing part of this incremental value with the customer, in essence, a supplier creates value for the customer.

Suppose we set Price$_f$ at Value$_a$. In this case, we would be giving all the incremental value to the customer as incentive to purchase Offering$_f$, with the relatively small remainder as the firm's profit. Contrast this with the alternative in which we set Price$_f$ relatively close to Value$_f$, so that we are giving only enough of the incremental value as customer incentive to purchase to maintain the inequality of equation 7-1.

The first alternative is sometimes called a *penetration pricing strategy* because the firm intends to make its overall profit through selling a larger number of units at a lower profit per unit. The second alternative is sometimes called a *skimming pricing strategy* because the firm intends to make its overall profits through selling fewer units at a higher profit per unit.

A number of factors can support pursuing penetration strategy versus skimming strategy, such as the market size and forecasted growth, anticipated learning effects (e.g., experience curve or market knowledge), anticipated reactions by present or potential competitors, and how persuasively demonstrable the value proposition is. The fundamental consideration that we want to emphasize, though, is that pricing strategy can only be understood within the context of the business unit's market strategy for each segment.

Furthermore, underlying the choice of a pricing strategy is the recognition that prospective customers vary in the value they place on a supplier's market offering and that this value may change over time. So, although we conceptually represent Value$_f$ and Value$_a$ as point estimates in equation 7-1 and figure 7-3, when we broaden our consideration from a single prospective customer firm to a market segment, these points become mean estimates of value distributions for all prospective customers in that segment.

As we move Price$_f$ closer to Value$_a$, customer incentive to purchase Offering$_f$ over Offering$_a$ passes the purchase threshold for a larger proportion of the distribution of prospective customers. That is, a greater number of those customers whose value for Offering$_f$ is less than the mean Value$_f$ will still have the inequality of equation 7-1 satisfied (using the individual Value$_f$ for their own firms).

Pricing Tactics

In contrast to pricing strategy, pricing tactics focus on shifting the supplier's position within the existing price range and may be transitory in nature. Typically, to gain the order, firms offer various discounts, rebates, reductions, and allowances to customers during the final negotiations.

For example, the supplier might use the pricing tactic of an initial-use discount, which appears as a price reduction on the invoice. It is an additional inducement for change or compensation for perceived or actual switching costs that the customer will incur. The initial-use discount has the advantage of establishing in the customer's mind what the supplier believes is the equitable price for the value of the offering—one that the customer should expect to pay on subsequent purchase occasions. Trade-in allowances, another form of initial-use discounts, are credits a customer firm receives from a new supplier in exchange for that customer's used equipment or unused supplies.

Suppliers also commonly use a number of other pricing tactics. Early payment discounts allow customers to deduct a percentage from the invoice for paying within a specified number of days. Volume discounts provide lower unit prices in return for larger-quantity orders. Freight allowances are invoice reductions that compensate customers for transportation and delivery charges. Rebates or bonuses cover a variety of schemes in which suppliers provide money or additional products and services at no charge as a reward based on the amount of business a customer has done with the supplier during some time period.

Instead of price concessions, firms can also offer customers inducements with respect to the terms and conditions. These include such things as when and where deliveries are to be made, the nature of payment schedules, and the particulars of return policies, warranties, and installation procedures. For example, extended dating—when the customer gets an unusually long period to pay for its purchase—serves as another pricing tactic.

Suppliers gain a reputation of being firm, consistent, and fair when they show discipline with respect to the use of price rebates and service concessions as price tactics. We advocate that suppliers only offer price discounts that are tied to those customer actions that benefit the supplier in some way. Without this connection, price discounts or other concessions simply amount to giving value away. For example, customers might receive freight allowances on full truckloads of orders placed by certain deadlines. These requirements enable a supplier to lower its logistics and delivery costs. Customers not ordering full truckloads or not meeting the deadlines should not receive the freight allowances, and suppliers must not waver in implementing this policy.

Pricing Transactions

Finally, transaction pricing focuses on realizing the greatest net price for each individual order. While discipline in pricing needs to be enforced at the strategic level, the tactical level, and the transaction level, it is especially important at the transaction level, where many pricing strategies go awry. So a business's management should monitor transaction pricing, which focuses on realizing the greatest net price for each individual order.

Managers learn from transaction prices the extent to which the firm's pricing strategies and tactics have been consistently applied. To underscore the significance of managing transaction pricing, consider this: it has been contended that a 1 percent improvement in price, assuming no volume loss, increases a supplier firm's operating profits by 11 percent.[4]

The challenge of implementing the pricing strategy and tactics are better understood when companies examine what percentage of their transactions follows their pricing guidelines. First, senior managers are interviewed to determine the business unit's pricing strategy and tactics. Then a random sample of recent invoices is audited to determine what percentage conforms to what the managers said and what percentage does not. For example, at one division of a large multinational firm, it was found that 67 percent of the invoices were nonconforming.

What were the consequences? First, the division had six managers who, instead of doing what they were supposed to do, spent most of their time deciding whether to accept "out of policy" pricing requests from the field sales force. Second, invoice accuracy began to suffer because the "special" pricing granted sometimes was not adequately communicated to the accounts receivable personnel. This led to an increased incidence of invoice reconciliation and the costs and customer frustration that go along with it. Finally, this lack of discipline created an impression in the market that there was always a better price to be had—if customers adamantly demanded price reductions or knew whom to call in the division. Thus, the frequency of calls coming into senior management instead of the sales force increased, invariably leading to price concessions.

To monitor transaction prices, suppliers can apply three concepts. First, managers construct a *pocket-price waterfall*, which refers to all terms, discounts, rebates, incentives, and bonuses that a customer firm receives for a given transaction. Managers then subtract these waterfall elements from the list price to produce a *pocket price*, which refers to the revenue a supplier firm actually realizes from that transaction. Finally, for some relevant time period, managers construct a *pocket-price band*, which is the distribution of all pocket prices the supplier has realized from its customers for the offering. The width and shape of the distribution convey pricing consistency.

Further analysis will reveal such things as which customer segments receive the greatest discounts, customers' willingness to pay, and how appropriately field salespersons are exercising their pricing authority. Management can use the information on the pocket-price band and waterfall to improve its firm's profitability.

For starters, supplier managers drive sales and marketing efforts off the "tails" of the pocket-price band. They target customers at the high end of the band for more collaborative relationships. Specifically, they try to increase purchases within this desirable segment by offering these customers additional value-added services. Some suppliers devise and implement customer loyalty programs, in which the suppliers share an additional portion of the value of each transaction with targeted customers to sustain and build relationships with them. Year-end rebates or bonuses tied to purchases or growth in purchases are examples.

At the same time, managers try to get pocket prices at the low end of the band back under control by making relationships more transactional. For example, one company capped price exception discounts for customers at 5 percent and granted them only after managers completed specific volume and margin impact evaluations.[5]

As a final step, business market managers strive to reengineer the pocket-price waterfall. They do so by examining each pricing element's significance to individual customers and its impact on their own firm's profitability. In some cases, they might restructure the manner in which they present a price element to customers. For instance, managers might shift funds from a price element that customers no longer value, such as a co-op advertising allowance, to one that is becoming increasingly important, such as a year-end rebate.

Siam City Cement Prices Insee Tong for Value

How do firms in business markets practice value-based pricing? Let us consider Siam City Cement, which is Holcim's subsidiary in Thailand. Holcim, based in Switzerland, is one of the world's largest cement companies.[6]

Siam City Cement found that the regular multipurpose cement available in Thailand was not optimal for some applications, like plastering. Because of its hardness, multipurpose cement led to poor finishes on walls. Often, cracks also developed, which had to be later repaired and reworked at considerable cost. In response, Siam City Cement developed a special masonry cement called Insee Tong. It provided a better finish, smoother surface, and fewer cracks—all of which was valued by general contractors and property developers. It provided high workability, faster application, and less skin irritation for the mason, and it reduced carbon dioxide emissions and resulted in less energy consumption. While these three influencers—general contractors and developers, masons, and the environment—were important, it was the contractors who made the decision on which cement to use.

For the contractor, Insee Tong masonry cement would deliver a 29 percent savings over multipurpose cement. These savings could be documented as arising from three sources. First, because Insee Tong did not require an additional mixer and covered 10 percent more area, it led to material savings of 2.4 percent. Second, faster application led to 2.2 percent cost savings. And, third, less repair work resulted in 24.4 percent savings.

Given that the price of the multipurpose cement alternative was 90 Thai baht (฿) per 40 kilo bag, the question was what to price Insee Tong at. The skimming price strategy would have been to set the price slightly less than the 29 percent premium of the multipurpose cement, which would be ฿116. At this price, the customer would have been largely indifferent about whether it purchased Insee Tong or the alternative, though Insee Tong would still deliver some additional benefits, such as less skin irritation and a smoother surface.

The penetration price strategy would have been to set the price closer to ฿90, at which point all the incremental value would be surrendered to the contractor. Given that the cost of producing Insee Tong was lower than multipurpose cement, the company decided to be relatively aggressive and adopt more of a penetration price strategy. The price was set at a 10 percent price premium to multipurpose cement—฿99. At that price, contractors pocketed almost 20 percent in cost savings, which was a powerful selling point in helping convert them.

To highlight the premium price positioning, the product was uniquely packaged in a plastic sheet to enhance its look and increase convenience in transportation. Furthermore, the advertising strategy employed a new approach to selling cement in Thailand. Instead of the exclusive focus on functional benefits, the advertising implied the emotional benefits. For Insee Tong, neither strength nor durability were emphasized; instead the focus was on the smoothness of the plastered wall surface. It was the first time the word *nian*, which in Thai means "smooth," was communicated in an advertising campaign for cement. An analogy was made between talcum powder and cement powder, using an image of a woman applying cement powder to her leg.

An important element was ensuring that Siam City Cement's personnel clearly understood the Insee Tong business and appreciated the value the product delivered. The entire management team, sales personnel, and technical support staff had to attend Insee Tong training classes. They were required to plaster a wall with Insee Tong and a competitor's multipurpose cement so that they would have the confidence to tell the story of how their product was superior to competitors' traditional cement.

The marketing program to introduce Insee Tong had to reinforce the value story in an extremely price-conscious market. Customers had to be convinced to move from the traditional thinking in terms of price per kilo and price per bag to the new value approach of thinking in terms of cost per square meter. And they had to experience the cost savings from Insee Tong to change eighty years of the established industry practice of using multipurpose cement for plastering. To achieve this, Siam City Cement presented fifteen metric tons of Insee Tong, at an initial-use discount of 100 percent (i.e., at no charge), to a leading real estate development company for plastering one of its luxury projects under construction. This allowed the developer to calculate all the cost savings in its own setting. This developer subsequently became the first customer of Insee Tong and served as a reference customer for other developers. As the most demanding developers adopted Insee Tong, a list of reference projects for each target market was compiled to be used for prospects. During this initial phase of focusing on premium projects, the strategy was to create a "pull" effect—that is, getting developers to specify use of Insee Tong with general contractors.

Siam City Cement also took steps to ensure that resellers' pricing on Insee Tong transactions conformed to the set pricing strategy and tactics. The company first introduced the product by giving it only to those resellers that would sell it as a premium product. This tactic was to show potential resellers that the company was serious about the premium price and the additional channel margin. Early on, though, one reseller did deviate from this pricing, selling Insee Tong at a lower price to meet that of a competitor's product. Siam City Cement held firm and cut the supply of Insee Tong to the reseller. The reseller was upset, but the supplier resumed deliveries a month later only after the reseller agreed to sell the product at the premium price point and accept the higher margin per bag.

During the first six months after the introduction of Insee Tong, Siam City Cement's salespeople regularly visited the housing development projects in their provinces to check on how the product was performing and on what wholesale prices the contractors were paying. This gave the company information on how Insee Tong was actually performing on-site and on whether its resellers were maintaining prices at the agreed premium. It took corrective action quickly against any resellers that gave prices lower than ฿99. It also learned that some resellers that understood the higher value of Insee Tong were able to sell it at a slightly higher price point. It rewarded those resellers with gold chains once they hit the target volume at the higher prices!

Insee Tong was introduced in March 2003. In 2003, the total volume of Insee Tong sold was 170,000 tons—despite the fact that two competitors introduced masonry cement at lower prices that same year. In 2004, the masonry cement market grew to 550,000 tons, with Insee Tong holding a 50 percent market share.

In 2005 and 2006, the masonry cement market continued to grow to 630,000 and 730,000 tons respectively, while Insee Tong continued to hold on to almost a 50 percent market share. During that two-year period, the price of masonry cement eroded as competitors used price as a competitive tool to win market share. However, Insee Tong still maintained its price premium over multipurpose cement as well as over competitors' masonry cement.

EIGHT

Prosper in Business Markets

Being a Value Merchant

EXPERIENCED general managers, vice presidents of marketing, and vice presidents of sales know just how difficult it is to prosper in today's business markets. And, when businesses *are* able to achieve superior sales growth and superior profitability relative to their industry peers, sustaining such success over time is extraordinarily difficult. We contend that customer value management can make a significant difference in a business's chances of prospering in business markets. We depict our customer value management processes again in figure 8-1.

In this concluding chapter, we provide evidence of the contribution that customer value management can make to superior business performance. We then consider how businesses can get started in implementing customer value management. We finish by discussing how businesses can continue to provide superior value and profit from it.

FIGURE 8-1

Customer value management processes

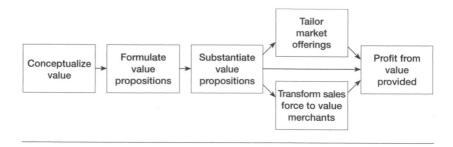

Achieving Superior
Business Performance

Customer value management contributes to superior business performance in two distinct ways. First, it is a methodical approach for gaining insights into changes in market offerings that target customers would value. Second, through demonstrating and documenting the superior value that the market offerings do deliver, customer value management enables suppliers to gain a better return on that superior value. Yet it is not a panacea, nor does outstanding customer value management alone ensure superior business performance.

Customer value management is an enabler, not a substitute, for technical prowess. Insights into changing market offerings to improve their value, for example, are of little use if a business and its suppliers lack the technical capability to create and produce the offering customers would value. Similarly, customer value management is an enabler, not a substitute, for implementation prowess. Discovering what services customers would be willing to pay extra for, for example, is of little use if a business is not able to deliver them consistently or when customers need them.

Evidence about the contribution of customer value management to superior business performance comes from two successively broader kinds of measures. First, there are specific market results for a business unit, such as its share of a customer's business, the profitability of that business, market share, and financial performance of the market segment. Second, there are company performance measures, such as growth in sales and percentage gross margin.

Business Unit Market Results

Evidence about superior business performance that comes from business unit market results can be more informative. Why? First, if a business is part of a very large firm, other units may not be practicing customer value management. So results from the specific business provide the most direct evidence of success. Second, some firms are privately held, so they do not report company performance measures that publicly traded firms must report.

Table 8-1 lists the market results provided as proof points at various places in previous chapters. We can add to this evidence the results for Composites One, which is privately held. Composites One has increased total gross margin dollars as a percentage of sales from 13 percent to 16 percent, which is outstanding in comparison to its industry peers in both absolute amount and overall growth. Further, Akzo Nobel's High Purity Metal Organics business has achieved revenue growth of 35 percent, compared to 15 percent for the industry, while maintaining its price premium.

Company Performance Measures

Providing evidence of the contribution of customer value management to company performance measures is even more difficult. To begin with, many of our examples have come from businesses that are part of large, multibusiness corporations. As a result, the financial accounting information that is available from

TABLE 8-1

Evidence of superior business performance: Market results reported in previous chapters

Business	Market result	Chapter
Intergraph	Revenue grew 35% per year versus 10–12% for the industry, and the company earned a profit margin of 26% versus 14–16% for the industry.	2
A leading resin supplier	The company received a 40% price premium for its new resin over the traditional resin product.	4
Orange Orca's polymer client	The client's salespeople began to close more business at a higher price per ton for the new Transplast polymer.	4
Rockwell Automation	The salesperson finalized a customer's order for 32 screw-drive pump solutions.	4
Grainger	The firm saw a sevenfold increase in sales to Pharma Labs in one year (from $50,000 to $350,000) and then nearly doubled sales during the next year (to $650,000).	4
Akzo Nobel Industrial Coatings	The company initially lost some customers, but it stabilized its sales volume while earning significantly better profitability.	5
Dow Corning and Xiameter	Xiameter contributed significantly to an increase in Dow Corning sales (from $2.4 billion in 2001 to $3.9 billion in 2005) and to an increase in profitability (from a $28 million loss in 2001 to a $500 million profit in 2005).	5
SKF	Salespeople were able to sell more products and increase the close rate dramatically, up to 50–60%.	6
Intergraph	Intergraph won new business with Aramco, an influential firm in the Middle East, which led to new business with Sabic, another major firm in the region.	6
Milliken	In the span of five years, Milliken registered record revenue growth and a significant increase in profits.	6
Sonoco's industrial products division	Sonotube forms with RainGuard technology received up to a 20% price premium over generic products and a 5% price premium over previous Sonotube forms, garnering the company a 16% increase in sales.	7
Seghers	Seghers won 100% of a customer's business at its profitable older plant and left unattractive business at its new plant for competitors.	7
Milliken performance products division	In return for significant cost reductions, a customer made Milliken its single-source supplier. Millikin then gained from the customer's increase in market share.	7
Eastman Chemical	The firm improved its profitability by eliminating an identified value drain and passed a portion of the savings on to the customer.	7
Tata Steel	Tata lowered its costs by eliminating a step in a process in one case and gained a price premium for customized lengths that more than covered its incremental costs in another case.	7
Quaker Chemical	The company received a 75% increase in the unit price of a product and a 10% increase in gross margin.	7
Siam City Cement	Despite competitors' price cuts, Insee Tong held a 50% market share in a growing market at premium prices.	7

company financial statements is far too general to meaningfully derive specific performance insights. Moreover, financial accounting information, while useful for reporting purposes, contains many items that do not fall under the responsibility of marketing or sales (e.g., leasing arrangements, depreciation schedules, acquisitions and mergers, taxation). As a result, bottom-line numbers often do not accurately reflect the contributions of initiatives such as customer value management. Ideally, we could draw on managerial accounting information from the business unit or even from the market offering by customer segment levels to more accurately gauge the contribution of customer value management to superior business performance. Because of its proprietary nature, though, businesses understandably are unwilling to share this information with outsiders.

Thus, we can offer only limited evidence of the contribution of customer value management for company performance measures. Companies that are relatively small or that are more focused in their scope provide the best sources of evidence. We also try to provide this evidence in the context of comparisons with industry peers.[1]

Applied Industrial Technologies increased its sales in 2005 by 13.2 percent versus 10.1 percent for its industry, while its gross margin was 29.2 percent compared with 25.5 percent for the industry. Grainger provides further evidence of sales growth and profitability. During the five years from 2001 to 2005, Grainger's annual growth rate for sales was 2.1 percent versus an industry average of 0.6 percent. Its gross margin in 2005 was 39.1 percent in comparison with 23.1 percent for the industry.

Kennametal had sales growth of 16.9 percent in 2005 versus 8.4 percent for its industry. Its gross margin in 2005 was 34.2 percent compared with 24.8 percent for its industry. Quaker Chemical had sales growth of 5.8 percent in 2005 compared with an industry average of 3.8 percent. Its gross margin in 2005 was 40.8 percent versus an industry average of 39.7 percent.

Tata Steel had sales growth of 43.8 percent in 2005 versus 39.8 percent for the industry. Its gross margin in 2005 was 39.6 percent compared with the industry average of 23.8 percent.

Finally, we have previously provided evidence of customer value management's contribution to company performance for two companies: Sonoco and Intergraph. As we related in chapter 1, Sonoco has been able to achieve the overall growth goal that senior management set, in part, through its use of customer value management and distinctive value propositions. It has averaged double-digit growth in sales (10.1 percent) and in profitability (18.7 percent) over the past three years. As we relate in chapter 2 and in table 8-1, Intergraph has revenue growth of 35 percent per year compared to 10–12 percent for its industry, while it has a profit margin of 26 percent compared with 14–16 percent for its industry.

Getting Started with Customer Value Management

Even recommending change in businesses is difficult. Skepticism abounds. Although we have provided examples of businesses that practice customer value management in a wide variety of industries and countries, most managers in business markets remain convinced of two so-called facts. First, their business is not like any other business. And, second, they have it more difficult in their business than does any other business![2]

As all experienced managers can understand, achieving enduring change in any business is extremely difficult. And it takes longer than anyone would like it to. But can a business change its culture from A to Z in one step? Specifically, can businesses that act as value spendthrifts suddenly become value merchants? In our experience, businesses cannot jump from A to Z in one step; in fact, they cannot even jump from A to B! Most often, they must move from A to A', and maybe even A", before they get to B. But the good news is that once they are able to move to B, they begin to pick up momentum, going from B to E, to K, and then to Z. How can businesses make this initial change and then speed up the pace to more quickly become value merchants?

No matter how successful customer value management has been elsewhere, some initial success in the business is necessary to counteract skepticism and convince managers that it has potential for their business. After that initial success, management must build on it.

Generating Initial Success

To demonstrate the viability of customer value management for their business, we counsel the general manager, and senior marketing and sales executives to engage in a customer value management pilot program. Businesses often make the mistake, though, of pursuing only a single project as a pilot program. This severely limits their learning as well as their chance for success. Instead, for a broader experience and greater understanding of customer value management and its potential, businesses should engage in a pilot program in which they tackle three to five business issues.

A customer value research project is defined for each issue, determining the scope of the project, the definition of success, and the composition of the team that will carry out the customer value research to address the issue. Engaging in three to five projects provides a basis for comparison and learning from the observed variation in project implementation and outcomes, helping participants understand why customer value management worked significantly better in some projects than in others.

Customer value management requires time and money, from which senior management seeks significant returns in incremental profitability, knowledge and skill acquisition, and the cultural change necessary to becoming a value merchant. The scope of each project needs to be sufficiently defined so that the customer value research can be conducted over a three- or four-month period. It is unwise to overwhelm teams with projects that demand more time than is reasonably available or to schedule projects that last more than six months. When the nature of the business issue is sufficiently broad or complicated, it is better to conceptualize it as a series of phases, each of which will take six months to complete.

Senior management must define at the outset what its expectations of success are for each project. A business case for change that results in $1 million of incremental profitability within twelve months is commonly defined as the principal goal of a project. This represents a relatively quick and attractive financial return on the resources that a business commits to each pilot project, while also reaping the knowledge and skills necessary to practice customer value management. It also ensures that the projects are addressing business issues of sufficient magnitude yet can be accomplished within the established time frame.

To gain a chance of adoption in a business, the customer value research projects have to generate *success stories*. These persuasively recount the significant gains in knowledge and profitability that have resulted from the projects. While learning what customers value is an important project outcome, to effect cultural change, the projects must lead to greater profitability—that is how businesses ultimately keep score. The business cases for change, which we discussed in chapter 4, detail the learning that has occurred and the subsequent changes that the business should make to gain incremental profit.

To have the best chance of generating success stories, senior management should take care in selecting the projects and making certain that team leaders and members have sufficient time to carry them out. All too often, senior management accepts what product managers or others who are proposing projects tell them without challenging how this is known or what data there is to support the claims. To hear most product managers tell it, their offerings have so many features that are different from competitors' offerings that customers want! Senior management should select those projects where there is evidence that the offerings have points of difference that will be valuable to target customers. The goals of each project then become to provide specific estimates of the value in monetary terms of these points of difference and to learn how these estimates vary across two segments of interest.

As we mentioned in chapter 4, the team leader may spend up to half of his or her time on the project, and team members may invest up to a quarter of their time. With everyone being so pressed for time anyway nowadays, it would seem obvious that teams' nonproject workloads should be lightened during the projects. Yet, as we have seen repeatedly, senior management neglects to take this issue seriously, which leads to even more stressed and overworked teams. The deleterious effects on the project outcomes and the teams' enthusiasm for customer value management are predictable. Customer value management has been most successful in those cases in which senior management has recognized the commitment necessary and taken steps to free up ample time for team leaders and members to do the work.

When senior management finds the business cases that the teams present to be persuasive and approves them, an implementation phase begins that we call *value realization*. The purpose of this phase is to ensure that the business delivers on the superior value estimated in the customer value research and on the incremental profitability detailed in the business case for change. This value realization phase is crucial; businesses that neglect to support it do not generate the success that they might otherwise have had.

A number of critical activities take place during value realization. The teams may need to gather additional data to refine or to extend the customer value models they presented to senior management. Further work likely will be needed on the action plans, particularly those that address implementation issues raised by senior managers. Value-based sales tools need to be created, or refined, if initial versions have been constructed in the business-case-for-change phase. Training needs to be devised to give the sales force practical experience using those tools, and supporting changes in performance review and compensation may be needed. (We discussed each of these in chapter 6.) A method of feedback should be put in place to audit the value that customers have actually experienced relative to what was promised them. This should be linked to the documentation of value we stressed in chapter 4. Finally, a system for tracking the incremental profitability realized should be put in place.

A final piece of advice for having the best chance of generating success with the pilot projects is to implement the customer value management process with integrity. What is the difference between good cooks and bad cooks? Good cooks always follow a recipe precisely the first time to see the results. Only then do good cooks improvise and make changes to the recipe to improve the results to suit their tastes. They then have a basis of comparison with their initial results. In contrast, bad cooks do not follow the recipe precisely the first time, instead improvising or taking short-cuts from the start. When the results do not turn out well, bad cooks have to ask themselves whether the results were due to the recipe or to the improvisations and shortcuts.

Our point here is that, at least in the pilot program, teams should follow the recipe closely, as we have laid it out in detail in chapter 4. After gaining good results, businesses may make changes in the process to adapt it to their specific setting and requirements. We have constructed every step in the process based on our experience with companies over the years that have implemented customer value management. We have found that short-cuts and improvisations during the process most often lead to diminished or compromised project outcomes.[3]

Building on Initial Success

After the initial round of projects in the pilot program has been completed, the team leaders, team sponsors, and others in senior management should contrast the projects that have been judged most successful with those that have been least successful. What can be learned? Do the most successful projects provide persuasive evidence of the potential for customer value management in the business? What are the shortcomings of the least successful projects, and what steps can the business take to minimize or eliminate them in the future?

Management should have value case histories created for the projects that it judges to have been most successful. These should be publicized in internal publications and placed prominently on the business's employee intranet. There should be recognition of the accomplishment of the teams generating these success stories. At the same time, variations in the value case histories and other learning gained from the successful projects (as well as learning gained from the less successful projects) can be translated into training materials that the business can use in the next round of customer value projects. These materials also can be used to expose a broader audience in the business to customer value management and what it might do for the business. Although some workers can relate to and learn from examples from outside their own business, others have more difficulty with this abstraction and strongly prefer examples generated from their own business.

Building on its initial success, the business typically will begin a second round of customer value research projects. This round might include a more speculative project or two than what was tackled in the pilot program. More speculative projects enable the business to extend its understanding of what customer value management can contribute.

Management will want to begin to develop experts in customer value management, so it may appoint the team leaders from the most successful projects in the pilot program to be either team leaders or team sponsors (if they have been promoted) for projects in the second round. Finally, management will want to begin to make customer value management a part of doing business. As an example, management may start requiring customer value research as part of its new product development (NPD) process. So, during NPD project reviews, senior management would expect the NPD teams to provide the points of difference for the new offering, the value word equations for each point, and value estimates from data gathered with target customers. As another example, product managers would be expected to provide the same kinds of support for any changes they recommend in the supplementary services, programs, and systems that augment the core product or service in offerings.

Continuing to Provide Superior Value

Customers have short memories for what suppliers have done for them while they have long memories for what they have done for suppliers. When a supplier achieves success through customer value management, its competitors will not stand idly by; they will respond by improving their offerings' value. Therefore, companies adopting customer value management must put in place systems to ensure that the value promised is actually provided (e.g., value documenters) *and* that this continues to be the case. They also must keep track of the cost savings and added value delivered over time and regularly apprise customers of this. They must further leverage their learning about how they have delivered superior value in particular customer markets by applying it to other markets. Finally, they must methodically work to find new or next-generation customer value propositions to pursue.

Making Use of Documented
Actual Value Provided

Through the process of documenting the actual value provided to customers, a supplier puts itself in a favorable position to discover further ways to add value or reduce customer costs. We call this "planned serendipity," because if supplier personnel working at the customer keep their eyes and ears open, they will notice chance occurrences that suggest potential ways of doing business better. Identifying value drains and value leaks, which we discussed in chapter 7, are good examples of such opportunities. Astute suppliers encourage and incentivize their technical service and sales representatives to notice and report customer incidents, utterances, or other observations that might suggest new ways of profitably serving customers.

Apart from this, by systematically keeping track of what has been done for each customer over time, in advance of the next contract negotiation, the supplier can frame what it has provided and what that is worth as a percentage of price paid. After all, the most common tactic by a competing supplier trying to win the business (back) is to offer price concessions. In such situations value merchants work to discover how close they must come to this competing supplier's lower price and still retain the business. Framing value delivered as a percentage of price paid enables a supplier to help the customer (and itself) better answer this question: what is being the incumbent worth? Is it being within 5 percent or 7 percent?

Why? Even after value assessments account for any specific, identifiable risks in using the outside supplier's product or service, the customer is still reluctant to change. Thus, to displace the incumbent offering, some additional portion of the value or a lower price must be given, a tactic that we call *incentive to change*. Without this incentive, purchasing managers are generally unwilling to recommend changing from the incumbent to another offering—even though they may threaten to.

Best-practice suppliers recognize that constructing and substantiating resonating-focus value propositions is not a one-time undertaking, so they invest in continually improving the capability of their people to identify what the next value propositions ought to be. SKF uses an innovative approach to gain and retain customers with superior value. In each contract period, SKF proposes a relatively near-term initiative, with a smaller but quicker economic return, along with a longer-term initiative, which has a potentially higher payoff. In the near-term initiative, the customer will realize the savings in, say, six months. The near-term payoff, although smaller, gets customer momentum and interest going in a positive direction, providing some tangible evidence to customer management that this approach is worthwhile, and sustaining interest and effort for the longer-term initiative with a higher payoff. Then, shortly before the contract renewal, SKF lets the customer get a glimpse of what it might do in the next contract period, again proposing a pair of initiatives: one shorter term and the other longer term with a higher payoff.

Quaker Chemical's unique solutions typically entail three- to five-year contracts for bundles of products and services that Quaker personnel deliver on-site. In a typical year, over 20 percent of Quaker's personnel work on-site at customer plants. In addition to providing service, personnel meticulously collect data on customer costs and benefits attributable to Quaker offerings. As part of its chemical management offering, Quaker has created a system, ChemTRAQ, that monitors the provision of its value-adding services and documents the resulting cost savings. Quaker personnel summarize these quantified cost savings and benefits as a scorecard or "delivered value proposition" in formal case studies, which they present on a monthly and annual basis to customer managers. The beauty of Quaker's value proposition design and refinement process is that it provides the tools (i.e., ChemTRAQ) and documentation (i.e., scorecards and case studies) that make it easy to track the company's performance and execute these agreements.

Leveraging Learning from Other Served Markets

Astute suppliers recognize that they can make use of learning from customer industries that they are serving to provide next-generation customer value propositions in other target markets. Although some adaptation may be required, the basic concepts about delivering superior value that have been successfully implemented in particular customer markets can have tremendous application in others. The challenge is to pull together the success stories from each of the markets served, provide a forum for sharing, and reward individuals for making successful adaptations. Quaker Chemical does a remarkable job in this.

Underscoring the contribution of value propositions to its business strategy, Quaker conducts a value proposition training program each year for its chemical program managers, who work on-site with customers and have responsibility for formulating and executing customer value propositions. These managers first review case studies from a variety of industries served by Quaker in

which their counterparts have executed savings projects and quantified the monetary savings produced. Competing in teams, the
managers then participate in a simulation in which they interview
colleagues posing as customer managers to gather the information
needed to devise a proposal for a customer value proposition. The
team that is judged to have the best proposal earns bragging
rights, which are highly valued in Quaker's competitive culture.
The training program, Quaker believes, helps sharpen the skills of
chemical program managers to identify savings projects when
they return to the customers they are serving.

As the final part of the value proposition training program,
Quaker stages an annual real-world contest in which the chemical
program managers have ninety days to submit a proposal for a
savings project that they plan to present to their customers. The
director of chemical management judges these proposals and provides feedback. If he deems the proposed project to be viable,
he awards the manager a gift certificate. Implementing these projects goes toward fulfilling Quaker's guaranteed annual savings
commitments to customers of, on average, $5 million to $6 million a year.

Uncovering New Value Propositions to Pursue

Best-practice suppliers put in place a process for finding potential
new value propositions to pursue and for shepherding them
through a systematic evaluation. These ideas might be for new
products, which are fed into an NPD process. Alternatively, these
ideas might be for valuable new supplementary services, which
are developed and provisioned.

*GE Infrastructure Water & Process Technology finds new
value propositions.* GE Infrastructure Water & Process Technologies' recent development of a new service offering for refinery
customers illustrates how its general manager allocates limited resources to initiatives that will generate the greatest incremental

value for customers and that those customers would be willing to reward the business for providing. The single largest cost for refiners is the oil that they refine. The most expensive oil per barrel is "sweet" crude, which has a low sulfur content. Crude oil with a higher sulfur content has a cheaper price per barrel, but during the refining process, the sulfur in it produces more acid, which is highly corrosive and thus destructive to equipment. Refiners could run their operations with crude that has higher sulfur content and a cheaper purchase price, but they hesitate to do that because of the potential damage it would do to the heat exchangers and other process equipment, which are expensive. Furthermore, refiners' biggest worry is reliability; an unexpected shutdown due to excessive corrosion in the refining equipment would be extremely costly.

Based on its detailed and comprehensive understanding of refinery processes and how refineries make money, GE Infrastructure Water & Process Technologies (W&PT) had a creative idea: if the business could develop a service that would allow refiners to use blends of crude with higher sulfur content, it could increase those refiners' profitability. The field rep submitted a new product introduction request to the hydrocarbon industry marketing lead for further study. (Field reps or anyone else in the organization submit new product introduction requests whenever they have an inventive idea for a customer solution that they believe would have a large value impact.)

Industry marketing leads, who have extensive industry expertise, perform scoping studies to understand the potential applicability of the proposed new products to deliver significant value to segment customers. They create a business case for the proposed new product, which are "racked and stacked" for W&PT's senior management team to review. The team approved this initiative out of a large number of potential initiatives competing for limited resources, and that led to the development of W&PT's Predator service.

Predator begins with an algorithm for refiners to blend different grades of crude and then predicts what would happen during the refining process. A detection system is part of the Predator service offering; its sensors are placed in key equipment to monitor the acidity levels, and then injectors feed corrosion inhibitors into the system. Although the customer purchases the algorithm, predictive model, sensors, and corrosion inhibitor chemical from W&PT, these incremental costs are far outweighed by the lower costs of purchasing cheaper crude. In fact, these price savings amount to five to ten times the price paid for the Predator service. Using its value generation planning process and tools, W&PT demonstrates what the potential savings to the refinery customers would be using Predator and then documents the actual savings produced relative to the incremental costs, thus realizing a compelling value proposition.

Value merchants find new ways to deliver superior value. One of the savviest value merchants we ever met was elected president of his industry association. In his president's address at this organization's annual meeting, he related to the audience what he was doing in his business to deliver superior value to customers. One of his competitors, somewhat flabbergasted, came up to him afterward and asked him whether he was worried about revealing what he was doing in front of all his competitors. "No," this gentleman responded, "by the time that your businesses are able to do what my business is doing now, we will be on to other things."

In relating this story to us, this gentleman told us that he had done this purposefully because it was better to have smart competitors than dumb competitors. He knew that if he could get his competitors to compete on value rather than simply on price, his industry as a whole would be better off. He also knew that true value merchants never stop finding new ways to deliver superior value to customers.

Relating Customer
Value and Price

How do customer value and price relate to one another?[1] To motivate this discussion, put yourself in the role of a customer manager, and consider the following scenario, which could apply to the acquisition of an electronic component. Then decide which product you would recommend that your firm purchase.

> *Your firm needs to make a decision about which of two alternative products to purchase: one offered by Supplier M and one offered by Supplier P. Based on two value analyses conducted by your firm, the value for Supplier M's product is found to be €4, and the value of Supplier P's product is found to be €6. The price of Supplier M's product is €1, and the price of Supplier P's product is €2.*

Which supplier's product did you recommend: M's or P's? Taking two alternative perspectives would lead to different decisions. Under a ratio comparison, you would recommend Supplier M's product over Supplier P's:

$$\frac{\text{Value}_m}{\text{Price}_m} > \frac{\text{Value}_p}{\text{Price}_p} \quad \text{(Eq. A-1)}$$

$$\frac{\text{€}4}{\text{€}1} > \frac{\text{€}6}{\text{€}2} \quad \text{(Eq. A-1a)}$$

Such a ratio comparison has been stated as the way in which customer value and price would be related to one another. As Gerald Smith asserts: "This almost always involves two dimensions of value: what the customer gets (benefits, savings, gains) and what the customer gives up (money, time, effort, opportunity cost). Most marketers combine these two dimensions in ratio form: Value = the benefits the customer receives relative to the price paid." Notice the overlooked commensurability issue in Smith's statements as well as his inclusion of price (indicated by "money") as part of value, both in contrast to our conceptualization.[2]

Under a difference comparison, you would make the opposite decision, recommending Supplier P's product over Supplier M's:

$$\text{Value}_p - \text{Price}_p > \text{Value}_m - \text{Price}_m \quad \text{(Eq. A-2)}$$

$$\text{€}6 - \text{€}2 > \text{€}4 - \text{€}1 \quad \text{(Eq. A-2a)}$$

Although Smith is probably correct that most marketers—at least marketing academics—embrace a ratio comparison, this thinking is misguided in two significant respects.

First, qualitative research with customer managers suggests that individuals are much better difference processors than ratio processors. Although we have chosen the monetary amounts in our scenario to facilitate comprehension of the differences between the two kinds of comparisons, division remains a more difficult mathematical operation than subtraction. Pick four numbers—a, b, c, and d—and try it for yourself, seeing how easy it is for you to divide a by b and c by d versus subtracting b from a and d from c.

Second, and more critical, difference comparisons are the way that businesses keep score on how they are doing. Simply put, they subtract the total cost of doing business from the revenue produced by doing business to determine the profit. While the ratio comparison for the scenario we presented leads to a decision to purchase Supplier M's product, would a customer firm indeed be better off by purchasing Supplier M's product versus Supplier P's product? Consider a situation in which the customer has a purchase requirement of a million units. Even though Supplier P's product has a higher purchase price than Supplier M's product (€1), this is more than offset by the superior value that Supplier P's product delivers (€2). Thus, a customer firm would have €1 million of incremental profit by purchasing its requirement from Supplier P instead of Supplier M.

In many cases, the values and prices for two competing offerings are such that the same decision would be made under either a ratio or a difference comparison. Nevertheless, as the scenario amply conveys, there are cases in which they would lead to different decisions. The overarching point is that most researchers, authors, and managers have not sufficiently thought through how customer value and price are related to one another nor provided rationales to support their assertions. The difference formulation in the fundamental value equation also enables us to focus on the value elements that matter (see chapters 3 and 4).

PeopleFlo EnviroGear Pump Customer Value Model

PEOPLEFLO Manufacturing has designed a new generation of hermetically sealed rotary pumps, which do not have dynamic shaft seals and therefore eliminate problems that shaft seal leakage causes. As a result, PeopleFlo's EnviroGear pumps not only satisfy customer requirements and preferences to reduce maintenance costs, but they also eliminate a source of environmental pollution at an affordable price. The target markets are producers of paints, resins, inks, and adhesives.[1]

Viking's dynamically sealed gear pumps would be considered the next-best alternative. When the PeopleFlo pumps and the Viking pumps are compared, four points of difference emerge: unplanned maintenance savings, planned maintenance savings, pump replacement savings, and leakage cleanup savings. A customer value model is built from value word equations for each of these points of difference, which can be estimated with usage data gathered at customers.

The value word equation and assumptions for *unplanned maintenance savings* are:

$$
\begin{aligned}
\text{Unplanned maintenance savings} = \Bigg[&\left(\begin{array}{l} \text{Number of} \\ \text{unplanned} \\ \text{maintenance} \\ \text{incidents per} \\ \text{year for Viking} \end{array} - \begin{array}{l} \text{Number of} \\ \text{unplanned} \\ \text{maintenance} \\ \text{incidents per} \\ \text{year for PeopleFlo} \end{array} \right) \times \\
&\left(\left(\begin{array}{l} \text{Average} \\ \text{worker} \\ \text{hours to} \\ \text{resolve} \\ \text{incident} \end{array} \times \begin{array}{l} \text{Worker} \\ \text{fully} \\ \text{loaded} \\ \text{wage} \\ \text{rate} \end{array} \right) + \begin{array}{l} \text{Average} \\ \text{purchase} \\ \text{price of} \\ \text{parts per} \\ \text{incident} \end{array} + \right. \\
&\left. \begin{array}{l} \text{Average} \\ \text{disposal} \\ \text{cost of} \\ \text{parts per} \\ \text{incident} \end{array} + \begin{array}{l} \text{Average} \\ \text{cost of} \\ \text{downtime} \\ \text{per} \\ \text{incident} \end{array} \right) \Bigg] \div \begin{array}{l} \text{Number of} \\ \text{like pumps} \\ \text{in service} \end{array}
\end{aligned}
$$

Assumptions:

1. Purchase price is a conservative estimate of acquisition cost.

2. Worker time saved can be productively redeployed to either preventative or predictive maintenance activities.

3. Worker time includes diagnosis, parts adjustment/replacement, and cleanup.

The value word equation and assumptions for *planned maintenance savings* are:

$$
\begin{aligned}
\text{Planned maintenance savings} = \Bigg[&\begin{array}{l} \text{Number of} \\ \text{Viking seals} \\ \text{replaced} \\ \text{as planned} \\ \text{per year} \end{array} \times \left(\begin{array}{l} \text{Average} \\ \text{purchase price} \\ \text{per seal} \end{array} + \left(\begin{array}{l} \text{Average} \\ \text{worker} \\ \text{hours to} \\ \text{replace} \\ \text{a seal} \end{array} \times \right. \right. \\
&\left. \left. \begin{array}{l} \text{Worker} \\ \text{fully loaded} \\ \text{wage rate} \end{array} \right) \right) \Bigg] \div \begin{array}{l} \text{Number of} \\ \text{like pumps} \\ \text{in service} \end{array}
\end{aligned}
$$

Assumptions:

1. Purchase price is a conservative estimate of acquisition cost.

2. Worker time saved can be productively redeployed to either other preventative maintenance or predictive maintenance activities.

The value work equation and assumptions for *pump replacement savings* are:

$$
\begin{aligned}
\text{Pump replacement savings} = \Bigg[&\left(\begin{array}{c} \text{Number of} \\ \text{Viking pumps} \\ \text{replaced} \\ \text{per year} \end{array} - \begin{array}{c} \text{Number of} \\ \text{PeopleFlo} \\ \text{pumps} \\ \text{replaced} \\ \text{per year} \end{array} \right) \times \\
&\left(\left(\begin{array}{c} \text{Average} \\ \text{worker} \\ \text{hours to} \\ \text{replace} \\ \text{a pump} \end{array} \times \begin{array}{c} \text{Worker} \\ \text{fully} \\ \text{loaded} \\ \text{wage} \\ \text{rate} \end{array} \right) + \begin{array}{c} \text{Disposal} \\ \text{cost per} \\ \text{pump} \end{array} \right) \Bigg] \div
\end{aligned}
$$

Number of like pumps in service

Where:

$$
\text{Disposal cost per pump} = \left[\left(\begin{array}{c} \text{Average} \\ \text{worker} \\ \text{hours} \\ \text{to clean} \\ \text{old pump} \end{array} \times \begin{array}{c} \text{Worker} \\ \text{fully} \\ \text{loaded} \\ \text{wage} \\ \text{rate} \end{array} \right) + \begin{array}{c} \text{Purchase} \\ \text{price} \\ \text{of} \\ \text{cleaning} \\ \text{materials} \end{array} \right]
\begin{array}{l} \text{Or:} \\ \text{outsourced} \\ \text{pump} \\ \text{disposal} \\ \text{charge} \end{array}
$$

Assumptions:

1. Purchase price is a conservative estimate of acquisition cost.

2. Worker time saved can be productively redeployed to either preventative or predictive maintenance activities.

The value word equation and assumptions for *leakage cleanup savings* are:

$$
\text{Leakage cleanup savings} = \left[\begin{array}{c} \text{Number of} \\ \text{leakage} \\ \text{cleanups} \\ \text{per year with} \\ \text{Viking pumps} \end{array} \times \left(\left(\begin{array}{c} \text{Average} \\ \text{worker} \\ \text{hours to} \\ \text{clean up a} \\ \text{leakage} \end{array} \times \begin{array}{c} \text{Worker} \\ \text{fully loaded} \\ \text{wage rate} \end{array} \right) + \right. \right.
$$

$$\left.\left(\begin{array}{ccc} \text{Price of} & & \text{Leakage} \\ \text{cleanup} & + & \text{material} \\ \text{supplies} & & \text{disposal cost} \end{array}\right)\right] \div \begin{array}{c} \text{Number of} \\ \text{like pumps} \\ \text{in service} \end{array}$$

Assumptions: same as for planned maintenance savings.

The *differential pump price* word equation and accompanying assumption are:

$$\begin{array}{c} \text{Differential} \\ \text{pump} \\ \text{price} \end{array} = \left(\begin{array}{ccc} \text{Viking} & & \text{Expected} \\ \text{pump} & \div & \text{number} \\ \text{price} & & \text{of years} \\ & & \text{in} \\ & & \text{service} \end{array}\right) - \left(\begin{array}{ccc} \text{PeopleFlo} & & \text{Expected} \\ \text{pump} & \div & \text{number} \\ \text{price} & & \text{of years} \\ & & \text{in} \\ & & \text{service} \end{array}\right)$$

Assumption: the PeopleFlo pump's expected lifetime is based on accelerated-use tests.

Finally, as in any customer value model, there are value placeholders, which hold the place for value that is yet to be determined. With EnviroGear pumps compared to Viking pumps, there are two:

1. EnviroGear pumps provide environmental stewardship through reduced fugitive emissions, reduced worker exposure, and potential reduced disposal of hazardous materials.

2. EnviroGear pumps eliminate or significantly reduce the hassle of unplanned maintenance and leakage cleanups (i.e., a social benefit).

NOTES

Chapter 1

1. Lisa M. Ellram, "Total Cost of Ownership: An Analysis Approach for Purchasing," *International Journal of Physical Distribution & Logistics* 25, no. 8 (1995): 4–23; and Marc Wouters, James C. Anderson, and Finn Wynstra, "The Adoption of Total Cost of Ownership for Sourcing Decisions: A Structural Equations Analysis," *Accounting, Organizations and Society* 30 (2005): 167–191.

2. Two articles that have advocated this kind of approach are: Thomas H. Davenport, "Competing on Analytics," *Harvard Business Review*, January 2006, 98–107; and Jeffrey Pfeffer and Robert I. Sutton, "Evidence-Based Management," *Harvard Business Review*, January 2006, 62–74.

Chapter 2

1. This section is adapted from James C. Anderson, "From Understanding to Managing Customer Value in Business Markets," in *Rethinking Marketing: Developing a New Understanding of Markets*, ed. H. Håkansson, D. Harrison, and A. Waluszewski (London: John Wiley, 2004), 137–159. © 2004. Copyright John Wiley & Sons Limited. Reproduced with permission.

2. Bradley T. Gale, *Managing Customer Value* (New York: Free Press, 1994), xiv (emphasis in original); Robert J. Dolan and Hermann Simon, *Power Pricing: How Managing Pricing Transforms the Bottom Line* (New York: Free Press, 1996), 9; Gerald E. Smith, "Segmenting B2B Markets with Economic Value Analysis," *Marketing Management*, March 2002, 36; and Thomas T. Nagle and Reed K. Holden, *The Strategy and Tactics of Pricing*, 3rd ed. (Upper Saddle River, NJ: Prentice Hall, 2002), 74 (emphasis in original).

3. James C. Anderson and James A. Narus, *Business Market Management: Understanding, Creating, and Delivering Value*, 2nd ed. (Upper Saddle River, NJ: Pearson Prentice Hall, 2004), 6 (emphasis in original).

4. For a recent example of where price is considered a part of customer value, see David D. Swaddling and Charles Miller, "From Understanding to Action," *Marketing Management*, July–August 2004, 31–35.

5. Lawrence D. Miles, *Techniques of Value Analysis*, 3rd ed. (Washington, DC: Lawrence D. Miles Value Foundation, 1989).

6. For more on points of parity and points of difference in a brand-building context, see Kevin Keller, Brian Sternthal, and Alice Tybout, "Three Questions You Need to Ask About Your Brand," *Harvard Business Review*, September 2002, 80–86.

7. James C. Anderson, James A. Narus, and Wouter van Rossum, "Customer Value Propositions in Business Markets," *Harvard Business Review*, March 2006, 90–99.

Chapter 3

1. W. Chan Kim and Renée Mauborgne, "Value Innovation: The Strategic Logic of High Growth," *Harvard Business Review*, January–February 1997, 102–112; and W. Chan Kim and Renée Mauborgne, "Creating New Market Space," *Harvard Business Review*, January–February 1999, 83–93.

2. The Medco example is from V. Kasturi Rangan, *Transforming Your Go-to-Market Strategy: The Three Disciplines of Channel Management* (Boston: Harvard Business School Press, 2006). The NetJets and Bloomberg examples are from W. Chan Kim and Renée Mauborgne, *Blue Ocean Strategy: How to Create Uncontested Market Space and Make the Competition Irrelevant* (Boston: Harvard Business School Press, 2005). The Dell example is from Nirmalya Kumar, *Marketing as Strategy: Understanding the CEO's Agenda for Driving Growth and Innovation* (Boston: Harvard Business School Press, 2004).

3. Francis J. Gouillart and Frederick D. Sturdivant, "Spend a Day in the Life of Your Customers," *Harvard Business Review*, January–February 1994, 116–125.

4. Axios Partners LLC is a strategic partner of James C. Anderson LLC in implementing customer value management at client firms.

5. Frank Joop of Intergraph, interview by authors, March 2, 2005.

Chapter 4

1. Most often, the supplier focuses the research projects on the market segments (or subsegments) in which it believes its offering provides value that's superior to the next-best alternative, with the intent of strengthening its offering's value still further. The research project might focus, though, on market segments (or subsegments) in which the supplier believes its offering presently provides less value than the next-best alternative. In these situations the intent of the project is to assess potential ways that the supplier could strengthen the value of its offering, making it superior in value to the next-best alternative. Finally, on occasion, the supplier might focus a research project on market segments (or subsegments) in which it presently does not have an offering, to assess what a potential offering would have to be to provide value that's superior to the leading offering in that segment.

2. James C. Anderson, James A. Narus, and Wouter van Rossum, "Customer Value Propositions in Business Markets," *Harvard Business Review*, March 2006, 90–99.

3. Orange Orca B.V. is a strategic partner of James C. Anderson LLC in implementing customer value management at client firms.

4. To learn more about the TCO Toolbox, go to www.tcotoolbox .com. Balder Electric has acquired this division from Rockwell.

5. Adapted and updated from James C. Anderson and James A. Narus, "Business Marketing: Understand What Customers Value," *Harvard Business Review*, November–December 1998, 53–65.

Chapter 5

1. James C. Anderson and James A. Narus, "Capturing the Value of Supplementary Services," *Harvard Business Review*, January–February 1995, 75–83; and James C. Anderson and James A. Narus, *Business Market Management: Understanding, Creating, and Delivering Value*, 2nd ed. (Upper Saddle River, NJ: Pearson Prentice Hall, 2004), chapter 5.

2. Anderson and Narus, *Business Market Management*, 187.

3. Robin Cooper and Robert S. Kaplan, "Profit Priorities from Activity-Based Costing," *Harvard Business Review*, May–June 1991, 130–135.

4. James C. Anderson and James A. Narus, "Selectively Pursuing More of Your Customer's Business," *MIT Sloan Management Review*, Spring 2003, 42–49.

5. Baxter International Inc., based in the United States, has split into two separate entities. Baxter Healthcare Corporation in this example and the following ones became Allegiance Corporation in 1996. Allegiance Corporation merged with Cardinal Health Inc. in February 1999 and is now known as Allegiance Corporation, a Cardinal Health company.

6. Michael V. Marn and Robert L. Rosiello, "Managing Price, Gaining Profit," *Harvard Business Review*, September–October 1992, 84–94.

7. Robert S. Kaplan and Steven R. Anderson, "Time-Driven Activity-Based Costing," *Harvard Business Review*, November 2004, 131–138. The time equation example comes from p. 135.

8. The corporate ownership of this business has changed. The business is now known as VWR Scientific Products.

9. Nirmalya Kumar, "Strategies to Fight Low-Cost Rivals," *Harvard Business Review*, December 2006, 104–112.

Chapter 6

1. Steven Kerr, "On the Folly of Rewarding A, While Hoping for B," *Academy of Management Executive*, February 1995, 7–16.

2. For more on involving salespeople early to gain their commitment, see Thomas A. Stewart, "Leading Change from the Top Line," *Harvard Business Review*, July–August 2006, 90–97.

3. Adrian Soghigian, Chris Spees, and Bruce Walters of Rockwell Automation, interview by authors, May 18, 2006.

Chapter 7

1. James C. Anderson and James A. Narus, "Selectively Pursuing More of Your Customer's Business," *MIT Sloan Management Review*, Spring 2003, 42–49.

2. Hermann Simon, "Pricing Opportunities—and How to Exploit Them," *Sloan Management Review*, Winter 1992, 55–65.

3. Shantanu Dutta et al., "Pricing as a Strategic Capability," *MIT Sloan Management Review*, Spring 2002, 61–66.

4. Michael V. Marn and Robert L. Rosiello, "Managing Price, Gaining Profit," *Harvard Business Review*, September–October 1992, 84–94.

5. Louise O'Brien and Charles Jones, "Do Rewards Really Create Loyalty?" *Harvard Business Review*, May–June 1995, 75–82.

6. Chantana Sukumanont and Siva Mahasandana of Siam City Cement, interview by authors, January 29, 2007.

Chapter 8

1. The source for this company performance evidence is Thomson One Banker, http://origin-banker.thomsonib.com.

2. Beliefs about these two "facts" remain in multidivisional or multisector firms when customer value management has been successfully implemented elsewhere in the company. Many managers, upon learning that customer value management already has been successful elsewhere in their own firm, have commented to us, "Oh, those businesses have it easy! We have it more difficult here."

3. Gabriel Szulanski and Sidney Winter, "Getting It Right the Second Time," *Harvard Business Review*, January 2002, 62–69.

Appendix A

1. This appendix is adapted from James C. Anderson, "From Understanding to Managing Customer Value in Business Markets," in *Rethinking Marketing: Developing a New Understanding of Markets*, ed. H. Håkansson, D. Harrison, and A. Waluszewski (London: John Wiley, 2004), 137–159. © 2004. Copyright John Wiley & Sons Limited. Reproduced with permission.

2. Gerald E. Smith, "Segmenting B2B Markets with Economic Analysis," *Marketing Management*, March 2002, 36.

Appendix B

1. James Anderson is an investor in and member of the Board of Directors of PeopleFlo Manufacturing.

INDEX

Note: page numbers followed by *f* indicate figures; page numbers followed by *t* indicate tables; page numbers followed by *n* and a number (such as 191*n*1) indicate material in endnotes.

ABOUT THE AUTHORS

JAMES C. ANDERSON is the William L. Ford Distinguished Professor of Marketing and Wholesale Distribution and Professor of Behavioral Science in Management at the Kellogg School of Management, Northwestern University. He is also the Irwin Gross Distinguished ISBM Research Fellow at the Institute for the Study of Business Markets, located at Penn State University, and a visiting research professor at the School of Business, Public Administration, and Technology at the University of Twente, in the Netherlands.

Professor Anderson's research interests are constructing persuasive value propositions in business markets and measurement approaches for demonstrating and documenting the value of market offerings. Among the more than forty journal articles he has written, five have appeared in *Harvard Business Review*, including "Business Marketing: Understand What Customers Value" and "Customer Value Propositions in Business Markets." He also has coauthored the book *Business Market Management: Understanding, Creating, and Delivering Value*, now in its second edition, published by Pearson Prentice Hall.

James Anderson also is the principal of James C. Anderson LLC, an international management consulting firm focusing on implementing customer value management at client firms. He has consulted and provided seminars for a large number of companies in North America, South America, Europe, Asia, and Australia, such as American Express, Arcadis, bioMérieux, Exxon Mobil, Femsa Empaque, GE, International Paper, Johnson & Johnson, Microsoft, Orkla Group, PPG Industries, and 3M.

NIRMALYA KUMAR is Professor of Marketing, Faculty Director for Executive Education, Director of the Centre for Marketing, and Codirector of the Aditya Birla India Centre at London Business School. He has previously taught at Harvard Business School, IMD (Switzerland), and Northwestern University.

Professor Kumar received his PhD from the Kellogg School of Management at Northwestern University. He has worked with more than fifty *Fortune* 500 companies in fifty different countries as a coach, seminar leader, and speaker on strategy and marketing. He has served on the board of directors of ACC, Bata India, BP Ergo, Defaqto, Gujarat Ambuja Cements, and Zensar Technologies.

A prolific writer, he is the author of *Global Marketing* as well as two other books published by Harvard Business School Press: *Marketing as Strategy: Understanding the CEO's Agenda for Driving Growth and Innovation* and *Private Label Strategy: How to Meet the Store Brand Challenge* (with Jan-Benedict E. M. Steenkamp). He has written more than forty cases and published four articles in *Harvard Business Review*—most recently "Strategies to Fight Low-Cost Rivals." Other of his academic papers have appeared in leading journals and received over a thousand citations. He has been the winner of several teaching honors over the years.

JAMES A. NARUS is Professor of Business Marketing at the Babcock Graduate School of Management, Wake Forest University, and a Distinguished Research Fellow at the Institute for the Study of Business Markets at Penn State University. He has also taught in executive development programs at Northwestern University, Penn State University, the University of Texas at Austin, and Texas A&M University, as well as in international management seminars at the Universidad Torcuato Di Tella (Argentina), the Copenhagen Business School (Denmark), Bordeaux School of Management (France), University College Dublin (Ireland), and Twente University (the Netherlands).

Professor Narus has written numerous articles on business market management topics. These articles have appeared in *Harvard Business Review*, *MIT Sloan Management Review*, *California Management Review*, and the *Journal of Marketing*, among other journals. Along with Professor James C. Anderson, Professor Narus is coauthor of *Business Market Management: Understanding, Creating, and Delivering Customer Value.*

Professor Narus has provided executive training seminars on management and consulting expertise for numerous corporations. Before his academic career, he worked as a market research analyst and fellow in the corporate marketing research division of DuPont.